Engaging in
Action Research

**A Practical Guide to Teacher-Conducted Research
for Educators and School Leaders**

Engaging in Action Research

A Practical Guide to Teacher-Conducted Research for Educators and School Leaders

JIM PARSONS
KURTIS HEWSON
LORNA ADRIAN
NICOLE DAY

Brush Education Inc.

www.brusheducation.ca

contact@brusheducation.ca

Cover design: Dean Pickup;
Front cover image adapted from presentermedia.com

Printed and manufactured in Canada

Ebook edition available at Amazon, Kobo, and other e-retailers.

Library and Archives Canada Cataloguing in Publication

Parsons, Jim, 1948-, author

Engaging in action research : a practical guide to teacher-conducted research for educators and school leaders / Jim Parsons, Kurtis Hewson, Lorna Adrian, Nicole Day.

Includes bibliographical references.

Issued in print and electronic formats.

ISBN   978–1–55059–449–2 (pbk.). – ISBN   978–1–55059–450–8 (epub). –
ISBN   978–1–55059–459–1 (pdf). – ISBN   978–1–55059–461–4 (mobi). –
ISBN   978–1–55059–465–2 (html)

1. Action research in education.   I. Hewson, Kurtis, 1974–, author
II. Adrian, Lorna, 1963-, author   III. Day, Nicole, 1973–, author   IV. Title.

LB1028.24.P37   2013 370.72   C2013-902686-X   C2013-902687-8

Produced with the assistance of the Government of Alberta, Alberta Multimedia Development Fund. We also acknowledge the financial support of the Government of Canada through the Canada Book Fund for our publishing activities.

 Government of Alberta ▪

 Canadian Heritage Patrimoine canadien

Contents

1

You as researcher

Why do many teachers and school leaders find research daunting?
How can this book help?

CHAPTER PURPOSE
To present research as a doable task

From "out there" to "in here"

Mention the word *research* to practising teachers—working diligently in classrooms with students—and you may hear something like this in response: "What have *they* learned *now* about what *we* should be doing?"

This response comes from a view of educational research as a mysterious exercise reserved for revered scholars in ivory towers who collect and decipher, and disseminate to the masses, information on *best practices*. This view thinks of research as scrupulous, lengthy investigations of far-off, unknown subject groups—as something *they* do *out there*, far from the realities of the classroom. Research, in this view, is the work of the academically elite and, although it informs and guides the work of teachers and schools, it still needs adaptation to the unique contexts and circumstances of each educational community.

Enter site-based, teacher-conducted research (what we call *site-based action research* in this book). More and more, educators are ripping down the curtains to expose the Great Oz, cutting through the mystification of research and finding value in study related directly to the everyday work they do with students and their colleagues. Educators, groups of educators, and educational systems are recognizing the power of conducting their own research—focusing with intentionality on specific questions and issues they face, and determining links between effective practice and student learning. Research, and the resulting *teacher professional learning*, has shifted *in here*, conducted with *real* students, staff, families, and community members. Rather than making sense of findings delivered by scholars and experts, professional teachers involved in site-based action research are engaging in meaningful study that has observable impact on those closest to them.

But I'm not a researcher...am I?

Consider the following profiles of some everyday teachers and school leaders. As you read them, allow yourself to think about how researchers could emerge from the backgrounds and desires of these educators. Can you see yourself anywhere in these descriptions?

Pamela: focusing on home reading

Pamela has taught in a number of primary classrooms over the past twelve years. Her colleagues affectionately call her classroom "the other library." Over her career, Pamela has amassed a sizeable classroom-reading collection that she uses with her students. She is a staunch believer that students should develop strong reading skills early in their school career, and, as a result, she implements instructional strategies and structures aimed at this goal. Over the years, she has begun to sense a decline in the amount of reading that students are doing outside of school. Didn't it seem like just ten years ago students were reading more at home than they are today? She is curious to see if her insight is more than just her singular perspective, and she hopes to help children read more and better. Are her colleagues also noticing the same trend? Has there actually been a drop in reading, or is it just a decline in the traditional practices that she associates with reading (such as curling up with a book alone or with an adult)?

Martin: flipping the classroom

Martin is the head of the mathematics department at a large urban high school. He works closely with six colleagues who share his passion for algorithms and problem solving. Over the past three years, this group has informally debated issues related to their individual instruction and the school's math program in general, often leading to sharing best practices and resources. The latest topic dominating their professional dialogue is the concept of the "flipped classroom": moving instructional components of teaching to online forums for students to access outside of class, and using class time for homework and practice with support from teachers and peers. Basically, the concept is to "flip" when teaching and homework happen. A growing number of schools are successfully using flipped classrooms, and the concept is interesting for this relatively progressive department. Martin is interested in exploring this concept with another member of the mathematics department, effectively developing a two-person team to investigate its merits. Could the flipped-classroom concept become a model for effective mathematics instruction in their department? Could it work for other subject areas at their high school? What have other schools done with flipped classrooms that has improved student learning? Finally, what should Martin and his colleagues do to get parents on board with a pilot of this innovative concept at their school?

Janice: a collaborative coaching model

Janice is an instructional coach. For the past four years, she has worked with teachers in a relatively small rural school district. Her role involves modelling lessons, supporting teachers with differentiated instructional strategies, designing assessments, and anything else aimed at improving teacher effectiveness across the schools she works with. Janice has found that she is most effective when coaching teams of teachers, rather than individual teachers. Although coaching individual teachers accounted for the bulk of her job in her first two years, she is now coaching more teams than individuals—and Janice has discovered that working with teams has led to greater collaboration within schools, more peer support that relies less on her involvement, and expanded coaching expertise at each site. She has also found that her time is more effectively used. She knows that most surrounding districts, and her colleagues in similar roles, still heavily focus on one-to-one support. She has begun to write about her experiences working with teams, rather than just individuals, on her professional blog. Other districts have approached her to lead professional development in this area.

Although Janice feels that she knows the benefits of team coaching, she is really interested to hear the thoughts of teachers she has worked with. Are they experiencing benefits from team coaching? Did those who received individual and team support have a preference, or feel that one method had a greater impact on their growth? What key elements, learned from coaching her colleagues, would be most beneficial to share with other instructional coaches?

Paul: a cross-district approach

At a meeting of district superintendents, Paul discusses the growing population of English-as-a-second-language (ESL) students with a group of four superintendents and associate superintendents. Each district has engaged in multiple strategies and initiatives designed to support this student population, but with varying success. Overall, the group's sense is that no one is successfully meeting the needs of their ESL learners. Rather than continuing to address this issue in their geographically determined silos, Paul suggests that the districts pool their resources to investigate the issue together, determining what practices really make a difference in schools across their districts and researching best practices from other jurisdictions. The informal group of leaders agrees to schedule a meeting to explore their "napkin idea" further, inviting the key personnel in each of their organizations to attend.

The professionals and situations we have described in these examples are not extraordinary. In fact, such inquisitive evaluations are happening in classrooms, schools, and school districts every day, involving practitioners such as you. Our experience suggests that education research—the systematic investigation of best practices, exploration of alternatives, and sharing of what "works best" with students and teachers—is increasingly something we, as educators, consider a regular part of "what we do."

However, a common response is: "But what I'm doing isn't research!" In other words, *real* research entails secret scholarly handshakes only shared with those in tweed jackets carrying recording devices and leather attaché cases; *my* research lacks the academic rigour of *real* research. Our intent with this book is to deconstruct the myth and mystique of educational research so that research fits more comfortably in the hands of teachers like you. We believe that your work as a researcher can have substantial impact on the greater educational community. So investigate, analyze, and share!

The rewards and challenges of research

Research, many tell us, is foreboding, like the spectre of Christmas Yet to Come. Research means facing the unknown. Even if you know what you want to do, there are lingering questions about how to do it. Then there is the writing-it-up part. For those of you who have not lived in an academic world of words, the task can seem like a test of your abilities. *Engaging in Action Research* offers a collection of ideas and processes that have worked for us and for practitioners like you. It contains step-by-step procedures that outline, from start to finish, your own research task. We hope this book helps you.

If you're reading this book, you are probably already grappling with that task. First, we offer some advice: take solace in the fact that many teachers, with similar background and abilities, have completed the task currently before you. In fact, you might be wise to go on a little field trip to look at the fruits of their labours. Read some research conducted by colleagues who worked in an area similar to yours. Second, we give you this promise: if you do your part, like those who have gone before you, you will be able to complete your research and share your findings. You will then know the secret handshake—but, of course, we can't tell you that right now.

You can do this

Whether you are a classroom teacher, school administrator, divisional coach, or district-level leader, you will be designing, conducting, and reporting a site-based investigation. You will be doing research. Many of you believe that such research is new, which can feel overwhelming. But in a way you have been preparing for this research for a long time. Research is less rocket science than carefully planned, rigorously attended activity. That means that if you have a good project (one worth doing) and you do it well (with care and consideration), you will be able to complete work that "contributes to the literature" (the defining feature of valuable research) and that you will be proud of. No one talks much about the pride of a job well done, but don't underestimate the motivational aspect of prideful work.

Our standard advice to new researchers is *don't get goofy*. Don't panic, or gratuitously waste energy. You need your energy and calmness of thought. It is one thing to enjoy a hike through the woods; it is quite another to be lost and wandering around in the dark forest. Think of this book as your guided hiking trail, and think of completing your project as a hike along this trail. It will sometimes be tiring, and you should know that up front. Perhaps at some point you will even feel like turning around. But if you know that you are not lost and that eventually you will arrive at the end of the trail, you will be able to look around and truly enjoy the vistas.

Engaging in Action Research is written to offer a brief, clear, and detailed look at how to complete your own self-directed, site-based action research. It provides a framework that will help you complete your own personal written report. The result will be dual: you will have contributed to the literature, and you will have engaged in professional growth. We wish you the best of luck moving from *out there* to *in here*.

2

Introducing action research

ESSENTIAL QUESTIONS

What do different research approaches entail?

How does your research purpose shape decisions about your research method and methodology?

CHAPTER PURPOSE

To deconstruct major terms and concepts related to research, method, and methodology

To examine factors that influence research methodology

We begin with a very simple fact: we do research to learn about something that is important or of interest to us. In its basic form, you've probably already filled your life with research activities but haven't named those activities "research." Perhaps you've read books on parenting to learn more about how to raise a child. Or, before you bought a car, maybe you visited several dealerships, asked lots of questions, and did some comparison shopping. Maybe you've been in charge of organizing a party at your school and have asked around to get some feel for what people would like to do. In other words, you have consciously set out to gather information for a specific purpose.

What it means to do research

All research, from highly structured formal laboratory experiments down to simple and informal inquiries, has these two characteristics in common: (1) there is a conscientious process at work that you (2) undertake for a specific purpose.

Research is *conscientious*: you are consciously aware that you are in a process of gathering information. This conscious process means that you've probably thought about the best ways to find out what you need to know, and that you are paying careful attention to the information as it comes in. Probably, you are organizing it—at least in your head.

You may even have done "researchy" things like *sampling* your population. For example, to plan your school party you may have decided that you didn't need to ask absolutely everyone to get a good feel for what people would like. Using your own discretion, you chose certain people to talk to. Then you asked them questions, and you listened to what they had to say. You did this "research" because their feedback was of direct relevance to something you wanted to accomplish—namely, to hold a party that everyone would enjoy.

This objective leads us to the second characteristic of research: it is *purposeful*. You don't invest time, energy, and care into gathering information unless you have a reason to do it. Your research process has a goal: to become a better parent, to buy a new car, to throw a good party. In this sense, all research is exactly the same. It may employ systems that seem much more complex, or may take on much broader or more esoteric objectives—for example, to find out what promotes student engagement, to improve student math marks, or to help new students overcome cultural barriers. But, at its most fundamental level, all research amounts to this: you want to know something and you work to find it out.

Further, the loftiness or humbleness of the research objective has little bearing on how we measure the success of a research task. A parent satisfaction survey at a junior high school is as "good" as a study of physically abusive children, or a focus group held among school division principals. Success is measured by the answer to one simple question: Did the research meet its stated objectives with accuracy and integrity?

Basic research, applied research, action research

As you can probably see by now, as researchers ourselves, we believe research can take many forms and have many different objectives. But research always has an objective. There are many approaches to classifying the types of objectives that guide research. They start with the answers to two basic questions:

- Is the research being conducted for the sake of gaining knowledge, or are its results intended to have some practical purpose?
- How broadly or narrowly can the results be applied?

One way to answer these questions is to sort research activities into two very broad categories: basic research and applied research (Organization for Economic Development and Cooperation, 2002).

Basic research

Basic research is undertaken simply to further knowledge. Because it is done for its own sake, it is not often seen outside of academic settings—although if you've ever picked up a book to learn about something "just because you're curious," you could say that you are embracing the spirit of basic research. In its formal sense, basic (or theoretical) research often involves proposing, testing, and developing theories. That is, its purpose is to provide principles that advance knowledge in a certain area of study. Theoretical researchers formulate and test models they believe may apply broadly to their disciplines.

For example, the human brain is the current focus of much educational research. How does the brain work? What can this understanding tell us about learning (and teaching)? Some researchers use an information-processing model of the human brain that compares the brain's functions to those of a computer. This theoretical analogy has become a framework for other researchers to build on. Over time, this theory has been used as a way of thinking about practical problems in applied research. Because it has been a useful model in a variety of circumstances, it has been accepted as a credible theory. This is actually the goal of most basic research: to come up with ideas, models, or paradigms that (with time and testing) come to be accepted as general truths or, perhaps more accurately, as generally valid ways of seeing the world. Simply put, the major objective of basic research is to have its findings apply as *widely and universally as possible*.

However, while theories generated by basic research provide us with helpful ways of framing problems and tasks, they do little beyond this "thinking" stage. For example, if we want to learn about *how* memory develops in young children, it is hardly helpful for us to simply announce, "Why, the human brain works like a computer!" and leave it at that.

Rather, we might use the information-processing theory to frame a particular study. We might say, "If the human brain is like a computer, where information is *processed* in short-term memory and *stored* in long-term memory, what can we learn about the strategies that children use to memorize their multiplication tables?" In other words, we *apply* the theory to a problem, issue, or phenomenon we encounter in the real world. This is where we get the notion of applied research.

Applied research

Unlike basic research, applied research does not have abstract, generalizable theories as its goal. Applied research has a context. For instance, an applied research study in education might look at the effectiveness of learning coaches on student participation. Another study might identify large numbers of struggling young readers in a school or district, and use what it learns to appeal for special program funding. A principal might hope to create faculty meetings that are more efficient and produce better decision making.

Of course, if an applied research study proves effective, it might be applied in other similar contexts and become "general" in that way. Patton (2002) suggests thinking of generalizability on a continuum (see Figure 1).

Applied research means that we learn about, test, and evaluate something we would like to use or apply (hence the name) in a real setting. Most research conducted in schools is concerned with practical ways to improve learning, so it is usually applied research.

Action research

Your research most likely falls into the category of applied research, too. Specifically, you probably want to study something you have encountered in the real world of education. The purpose of your study is probably to identify and propose solutions to very specific issues that have emerged from your own organization's context. In this sense, your research falls toward the far right of the continuum for specificity: it is very specific. This kind of research—often undertaken by teachers right within their school—is a special category of

Figure 1 CONTINUUM OF RESEARCH GENERALIZABILITY

BASIC RESEARCH	APPLIED RESEARCH
• abstract	• contextualized
• theoretical	• practical
• broad generalizations	• specific applications
more general ⟵	⟶ more specific

Table 1. COMPARING BASIC, APPLIED, AND ACTION RESEARCH

	TYPE OF FINDINGS GENERATED	PURPOSE OF RESEARCH	EXAMPLE
BASIC RESEARCH	• not bound by context • meant to be general • goal: wide application across situations	• to create principles, theories, or frameworks that someone else can apply to other research and problem-solving situations	• medical research on cell regeneration in plants and animals (which could be applied to research on treating Parkinson's disease)
APPLIED RESEARCH	• more specific to a context than basic research • somewhat generalizable across similar cases	• to understand and explain a particular type of problem or phenomenon	• coaching strategies for a junior high swim team that use basic research about adolescent psychology
ACTION RESEARCH	• very specific to a context • focus: problem solving • no impetus to generalize to other cases	• to solve specific problems within specific contexts using any combination of basic-research and applied-research strategies	• "How can workers in my particular organization be encouraged to feel a sense of ownership and pride in their work?"

applied research called action research. Table 1 summarizes how action research differs from basic and applied research.

Method and methodology

In the previous section, we talked about research objectives and presented ways to classify and think about what a research task is trying to achieve. Now we need to consider how we go about accomplishing these objectives. The next important stage in any research task involves method and methodology.

Factors in determining a research method

The term *research method* or *research plan* simply refers to a carefully laid out series of steps for finding out what you want to know. There are many ways to develop a research method, and methods are shaped by the nature of the question identified for research. Considerations that might shape your research method include (but are certainly not limited to):

Ethical concern for your research subjects: one of the most critical aspects of a research plan is ensuring that your work does not cause harm to others. All organizations that conduct research have ethics-review boards that examine research methods to ensure research subjects are protected from physical harm, psychological damage, or other negative effects.

The availability of data: research tasks may be constricted in some ways by limits on data. If you are researching infant behaviour, for instance, you obviously cannot ask the subjects to verbalize their experiences. Similarly, studies of the experiences of Holocaust survivors become increasingly restricted as these individuals grow old and die.

Time, money, and other resources available for your study: most research projects work within a set budget and time period, so the ideal set-up may not always be feasible. If nothing else, feasibility can force you to be creative about your research plan. One researcher we know, for instance, was unable to conduct a focus group because participants were scattered all over three school districts and could not travel. Instead, he set up an online discussion board. The messages from the board were a valuable source of data and, because they were already in written form, they did not have to be transcribed.

The amount of research that has already been done in the area: some research—in the area of leadership behaviour, for instance—is easier to structure and conduct because a large body of work and literature already exists on the topic. Where a wealth of work is absent, a researcher needs considerable personal expertise and resources to complete her research task.

How you want to use your findings: this is one of the trickiest factors that shape research methods. It is easy to collect data that do not truly answer the questions asked in your research. For instance, say that you want to study the effectiveness of an adult literacy program. You might gather data on program attrition rates or the reading levels of program graduates. But do these data really answer your question? Perhaps attrition rates have to do with factors outside of the program itself—maybe participants have trouble obtaining transportation to and from the program. Perhaps lower-than-expected reading scores by graduates do not capture whether the program has been truly "effective" in terms of transforming participants' lives.

Designing a research method is not a simple process. For this reason, research is both challenging and fascinating; the possible number of research designs is as unlimited as the number of research questions you could ask. Each research question is uniquely shaped by its goals and context and, in turn, each requires a unique approach in its method.

Method versus methodology

The terms *research method* and *research methodology* can be confusing and they are not interchangeable. *Research method* refers to the series of steps you choose to find the answer to your question—it is like a "research lesson plan." *Research methodology* is more like an overall guiding philosophy—it is your explanation of *why* you chose to approach the question as you did.

A clear methodology is important because it reveals the fundamental beliefs that you, as a researcher, hold about the question you are investigating. To fully understand your research, your readers need to understand the perspective you bring to your work. As you will see in our discussion about researcher bias later in this chapter, articulating your worldview in your research methodology lends context and understanding to your findings and interpretations.

Briefly, methodology is:

Philosophical: when we begin to examine our own or other researchers' methodologies, it is almost inevitable that we venture into questions about what reality is (metaphysics) and how something can truly be known (epistemology). You don't need to study philosophy to be philosophical; you may find yourself asking your own particular versions of these questions quite naturally if you are careful and reflective about your research work.

Normative: inherent in methodology are assumptions both about how the world is organized and how it *should* be organized. In the past, many researchers in the social sciences believed objectivity was key to good work. Today, most researchers believe that research cannot be objective or values-free.

Paradigmatic: in 1962, philosopher Thomas Kuhn proposed that scientific inquiry is shaped by great, sweeping paradigms or metaphors about how the world works. Collectively, our way(s) of seeing the world can be so entrenched, taken for granted, and constantly reinforced that it is almost impossible for us to imagine viewing reality any other way.

Quantitative versus qualitative research

In this introduction to action research, we will consider only two basic research paradigms: quantitative and qualitative (see Table 2 for a summary of the differences between them). These are broad categories, but they capture and represent many tensions and issues surrounding reality and how it is represented (philosophy is at the heart of research). Your decisions about methodology sort those tensions out and pin them down—at least temporarily, while you complete your research task.

The idea of defining a research methodology may appear quite daunting. In our experience, when most people think of research, they have intimidating visions of confusing statistical analyses, lengthy incomprehensible reports, and lab technicians poking rats. They believe academics can do it, but they cannot. The research you will conduct is nothing like this. In fact, most popular or common notions about what research is come from a quantitative research paradigm.

Quantitative research comes from Western intellectual traditions. Chiefly, it is empirical: it aims to "discover" through the senses experiences that can be measured. These measurements are used to break the world into small pieces and to study these separate pieces with microscopic rigour. In this sense, quantitative research is *deductive*: a "big idea" or general theory (which is usually stated in a hypothesis) is tested by looking at whether individual *facts* support it, and facts are those things that we can perceive with our senses and *count up* in some way.

When we count up these data, we are aggregating them: individual cases or responses are not so important. Instead, the data as a whole

Table 2. QUANTITATIVE VERSUS QUALITATIVE RESEARCH

QUANTITATIVE RESEARCH	QUALITATIVE RESEARCH
• measures phenomena	• describes phenomena
• is deductive	• is inductive
• studies the world in small, discrete pieces	• studies the world as an organic whole
• findings: often generalized to the larger world	• findings: often apply in specific contexts
• researcher: should be objective and unbiased	• researcher: acknowledged, and sometimes embraced, as subjective
• setting: controlled and artificial	• setting: natural

are analyzed for any significant patterns—this is where the statistical analysis comes in. For example, we might compare two groups, one of which received a program and one of which did not, when testing the effectiveness of a new teaching idea. Or, we might try to find a cause that links two phenomena together. Or, here's another obvious example: public opinion polls, which collect data and analyze them statistically.

Analyzing human experiences with statistics can tell us a great deal. For example, statistical analyses have generally found a correlation (a link) between low income and poor health. Although we might speculate *why* exactly this correlation exists, simply *knowing* it exists can be helpful. A new school in an inner-city neighbourhood might look at statistics such as household income to predict needs and services that might be important. Another school might look at demographic statistics and note that the population in its area is quite young. Based on this information, it might decide to develop early literacy programs.

Gathering such data is a careful process. Quantitative research uses specific procedures, or recipes, to conduct systematic studies. These procedures are carefully delineated so that others can repeat them under the same conditions. When the same procedures and conditions produce the same results each time, the phenomenon under inquiry is established as factual or *true*. Actually, we say that "the research supports the following hypothesis:...." We are highlighting words like *true* because this explanation is, of course, a simplified explanation. Proving something empirically is usually a lengthy and complicated process, and much of what is learned is still regarded with a healthy degree of skepticism.

As researchers, we do, however, reserve our *greatest* skepticism for the most complex and unpredictable of study subjects—human beings. *Qualitative* research recognizes that *quantitative* research—while generally a comfortable fit for the hard sciences—cannot always effectively capture the complexity, diversity, and subtlety of human experience. Much of what we are is maddeningly or wonderfully *im*measurable and *un*countable and therefore *un*quantifiable. It is like trying to count love.

Qualitative research comes from a very different paradigm than quantitative research. Generally, qualitative research explores social or human problems. It tries to describe a phenomenon (quality), not count it (quantity). To complete qualitative research, a researcher must build a complex, holistic picture; analyze words; report detailed views of informants; and usually conduct the study in a natural setting (Creswell, 2009).

We can compare quantitative and qualitative research on several fronts. First, as we noted, quantitative research is generally *deductive*: it proposes a theory and seeks facts to support or challenge the theory. Qualitative research is, by contrast, *inductive* or *emergent*. In other words, it stands the quantitative process on its head: the theory—or perhaps more accurately, the interpretation—*emerges* from the data. Such research is often referred to as *open-ended inquiry*, because the researcher enters the scene with an "I wonder what I'll find out" approach. While a guiding or focusing question or set of questions begins the process, it is common and acceptable for these questions to morph in response to what the research finds out along the way. This process stands in direct opposition to quantitative research questions, which are carefully constructed and must be answered directly for the study to be considered valid.

We have stated that quantitative research is empirical—a characteristic tied to science that is more Western and industrial/technical in its traditions. Qualitative research also makes use of sensory observations, but it can be more open to the felt or *subjective* experiences that empirical studies actually strive to eliminate or control by being as *objective* as possible. We might say that qualitative research is the East to the quantitative research of the West, the yin to the yang; qualitative research shows a receptivity to the nuanced, unique characteristics of a given problem or context.

One particular expression of this distinction is in the research *setting*. Quantitative studies carefully control the research setting so that it does not bias findings—in other words, contextual factors are, as much as possible, eliminated or neutralized. For qualitative research, however, context is what the study is about: the researcher wants to know how people behave, think, and feel in their own environments. Because qualitative research is holistic in character, it focuses on understanding the entire environment within which a research problem *lives* and tries to paint a complete picture of that context. The setting of the research is *naturalistic,* in that it "takes place in the real world…and the researcher does not attempt to manipulate the phenomenon of interest" (Patton, 2002). In fact, we often speak of *fieldwork* in qualitative research, using the term as it emerged from studies in anthropology and natural sciences (Bogdan & Biklen, 1992). The researcher is "in the field" when she is observing or interacting with participants in their own environment.

Because qualitative research relates to specific contexts, it is less generalizable than quantitative research. However, qualitative researchers don't aim so much for generalizable conclusions: the individual case is more important than patterns that might emerge from aggregating and generalizing the data.

ENGAGING IN ACTION RESEARCH

Which to choose?

Both major paradigms—quantitative and qualitative—have legitimate roles to play in research. The choice of one over the other (or in some cases, a decision to use strategies from both) depends on the research question to be answered. Either methodology could be used to study an issue—say, literacy—and each would produce very different kinds of information. Quantitative research might focus on the achievement of students on standardized tests. Qualitative research might focus on the *life worlds* of children who are creative writers, wondering about aspects of their family backgrounds that might encourage creativity and fluency, and so explain how these children came to think outside the box.

In some cases, we might use elements of both quantitative and qualitative methodologies in a research plan. If, for example, we were to gather statistical data on learner satisfaction with a literacy program, we might learn that 78% of participants were satisfied or very satisfied with the program. These are quantitative data, and they are valuable because they tell us that the program is doing a good job.

What they don't tell us is the impact of the program on individual children. Case studies or focus groups—qualitative research strategies that allow us to explore subjects in depth—might reveal insights that we could not gain from statistics. For instance, they might reveal that part of the program's success came from teachers who had particularly good relationships with the children and were exceedingly helpful to families, or from deeper, closer relationships that developed among staff through their teaching.

It is also worth restating that the differences between quantitative research and qualitative research are not always hard and fast. They are two paradigms, two different approaches to problem solving, but this does not mean that you must religiously adhere to one or the other (although some people do). Many researchers (ourselves included) take an eclectic approach to methodology, employing both quantitative and qualitative strategies where most useful.

The following examples may help further clarify what is usually referred to as a *mixed methods* approach.

Observing preschoolers

A researcher observing preschoolers in a playgroup uses an observation checklist, counting certain behaviours that he observes. For instance, on a given day he may observe and tally seven instances of verbal aggression and two instances of physical aggression. In each case, he jots down observations that he will later turn into rich descriptions of the playgroup setting. Here the researcher is observing in the field. This is a "qualitative-ish" strategy. However, the fact that he is also counting specifically defined behaviours leans more towards a quantitative approach.

Recreational program satisfaction

Another researcher is trying to evaluate the recreational programs at a high school. The main source of her data is a survey that asks students to identify which programs they have used, and to indicate on a scale of one to five how satisfied they were with each program. She also uses documents to review participation rates in the programs over the past five years. The data she is collecting are countable and therefore quantitative. However, she also includes open-ended questions on her survey so participants can respond freely with their own ideas—a qualitative approach. Although the bulk of her report will be drawn from the numeric data she has gathered, she will use participant comments to understand their experiences with the program.

In each example above, you can probably see that quantitative and qualitative research strategies can complement and support findings. We call this complement *triangulation*, whereby approaching the same problem from different angles (in this case, different methodologies) improves the accuracy and validity of the research findings.

Types of quantitative (statistical) studies

Experimental: usually uses a treatment group and a control group to study the effects of an experimental intervention. For example, a school might try two different reading programs with two groups of grade-one students, and compare the results that each program achieves.

Correlational: looks for associations between two phenomena. An example of a well-known correlation is the association between age and risk-taking behaviour. An important thing to remember about correlations is that they show only a relationship between two variables, not the cause of that relationship.

Causal-comparative: looks for the causal connection between two linked phenomena. What factors, for instance, might determine a child's level of physical fitness? A study might examine family history, eating habits, or other lifestyle factors. Establishing cause can be a chicken-and-egg problem: it is difficult to gain certainty.

Types of qualitative (descriptive) studies

Case study: focuses with great detail on a particular person or group. For instance, a highly effective school might be studied for practical lessons that could apply to other, similar schools. Description is important to case-study research.

Ethnographic: attempts to create rich portraits of everyday life. Ethnographic studies are similar to case studies in that they are highly focused and descriptive, but their flavour is different, and they put less emphasis on how the research will be used.

Hermeneutic: studies texts (defined broadly) to assess the significance of the texts for the people being studied. Hermeneutics focuses on understanding shared linguistic meanings of textual representations or symbols. In schools, texts may include things like mission statements, policy documents, or even the physical organization of a classroom (e.g., what is posted on the walls).

Historical: uses documents (or interviews) to study something that has occurred in the past. In school settings, such information can provide a valuable context for present-day concerns. For instance, revealing a lengthy history of a school's culture might help explain why it is resistant to change.

About bias: situating the researcher

Another important distinction between quantitative and qualitative methodologies is the role of the researcher within the research. Quantitative research is highly structured, because those who practise quantitative research depend on the careful application of specific procedures in an attempt to avoid human bias and therefore human error. The relationship between researcher and subjects is—at least as far as the research process is concerned—a nonrelationship because the researcher does not want her presence to influence or interfere with the *subjects* in any way. This is not to say that all quantitative research relationships are cold and robotic. But it does say that the researcher attempts to be more cautious and structured in her approach, and works hard to not allow any human relationship to compromise the research work.

As an example, say that a researcher is trying to determine what might influence aggressive behaviours in students. He wants to find out if teacher attitudes might influence these behaviours. After a discussion, the subject teachers fill out a survey that asks them to agree or disagree with a number of statements. To make sure the subjects address his specific questions only, the researcher must be consistent in his procedures. He will read the exact same instructions to each teacher, perhaps even using a script, and may not answer questions the subjects ask, so that no subjects have more insights than others.

Avoiding researcher bias in carefully controlled laboratory conditions seems straightforward, but life conspires to become murkier when we start collecting field data. First, avoiding bias isn't really viewed as a problem in qualitative research. Instead, human biases are acknowledged as important perspectives that must be understood. Within the qualitative paradigm, it is believed there can be no research without researcher bias. In fact, researcher bias is always present and can help the reader of qualitative research better understand how the research was done. For this reason, qualitative researchers often spend a great deal of time attempting to explain their biases at the beginning of their research reports. The rationale here is simple: the more you know about the person, the more you can understand the research.

Qualitative research acknowledges that bias exists and is not bad, which allows researchers more latitude in the types of relationships they can form with participants. Methodologically, it is not wrong to enter the subjective world of the research subjects; in fact, it is desirable. The best way to achieve understanding is to talk and spend time with research subjects, often participating in their daily lives in what is logically called participatory research.

For some, the element of bias in qualitative research—particularly in its more intimate and participatory forms—simply makes the research invalid or unscientific. Researchers are often chastised for imposing their own perspectives on what they study, and it is true that some research is simply too idiosyncratic to be useful. However, acknowledging and working with your biases doesn't mean you give your perspectives free rein in your research. The researcher's job, after all, is to represent the situation fairly and accurately. Responsible researchers do their best to be conscious of personal biases that shape their perceptions and their work.

Keep the goal in mind: improving students' lives

Many people (ourselves included) believe that the true value of research is determined not by arguing which research approach is superior (although academics often do this), but by returning to the question of whether a study furthers the objectives it sets out to achieve. It is easy to bog down in details and lose the big picture.

As an illustration, we recently heard a high-level civil servant suggest that the educational research being done in his jurisdiction should avoid a research problem called the Hawthorne effect. The Hawthorne effect basically says that we don't want researchers treating subjects as special and having the subjects learn more because of the special treatment. From a quantitative research perspective, this "extra learning" is a problem. But think about that for a moment: treating students as special so that they learn more is a cornerstone of excellent teaching. In fact, we hope we do this and do it well. Why would we want our research to avoid this influence?

Our lesson here is that a research method should serve the research objectives, not the other way around. In this chapter, we've discussed theoretical perspectives that offer a foundation for determining your own research method and methodology, but these perspectives should not alone shape your research: this amounts to the tail wagging the dog.

As we've emphasized, your research can draw on *different* theoretical perspectives and a *combination* of strategies, so long as it is conducted ethically, with your commitment to—as best as you can—"tell the truth" about what you are studying. The goal is to further knowledge about what improvements can be made in the lives of students in schools.

3

Starting a research plan

ESSENTIAL QUESTIONS

What steps does action research involve?

What will you need to consider in the planning stages?

CHAPTER PURPOSE

To provide a background understanding related to the action research process

To provide steps and guiding questions to assist in developing a research topic and defining a research question

A comment we often hear from new researchers is how daunting research seems in the early stages. It is one thing to read, collect notes, and synthesize ideas into a paper whose audience is a professor; it is another thing to take responsibility for a process that involves and affects real people in your organization.

We offer this encouragement: new researchers can and do successfully complete site-based action research. We assure you the process is doable, and you will be proud of your result when you have completed the work that is your research. The key (and this may sound trite, but it's true) is to take one step at a time. One goal of this book is to lead you—as simply and clearly as possible—through the necessary steps.

The steps of our site-based research model, as presented here, are a composite of various theoretical models of field-based research, and our experience researching and supervising scores of research projects since the early 1970s. Our goal is to foster understanding of the action research process—the approach, as a teacher, you will likely take in your research.

The action research process

Many perspectives and models are published about the action research process, and we will share a brief description of several authors' views. By doing this, we hope you get a sense of how inclusive and yet flexible this process can be. We believe any research that promises action and improvement within a school is acceptable, as long as it's ethical, helpful, and done well. We believe site-based action research provides optimum ways educators might make applied and lasting changes to the places where they live and work.

An action and reflection spiral

Action research can be viewed as a cyclical or spiral process that moves from reflection to action and back to reflection again. An action research project might have one or many iterations of a planning-action-evaluation cycle; often, it even lacks a definite outcome. In fact, action research is often viewed not as an isolated project, but as an ongoing philosophy of thinking, learning, and problem solving.

This ongoing, re-cycling process can appear odd because many of us are conditioned to solve problems in a linear fashion, ending with a definite resolution. However, if we consider the problems and relationships that characterize our lives, we realize that problems are rarely solved in a linear way. Why? First, problems are often difficult to define. Second, there is rarely one clear and obvious solution. Third, once resolved, issues tend to be far from over, and new problems or opportunities will emerge.

All the while, the process is witnessed and negotiated by different stakeholders with different values and perspectives. You might not read this in another book about research, but we believe research is primarily about relationships—relationships between people and people, between people and knowledge, between doing and thinking about doing. Action research recognizes that life's problems (and their solutions) are complex. So, we impose some order with a research process, but we remain flexible enough to accommodate what we learn. The following models are examples of action research processes that provide overall direction and shape for a task without being restrictive. You can use these general frameworks to think about the big picture in your own site-based task.

ACTION RESEARCH MODEL 1: ERNEST STRINGER

We, like many site-based education researchers, view Ernest T. Stringer as a guru of action research. Stringer (1999, p. 8) offers a methodology that can function as a basic approach to, or routine for, action research. His process is simple and flexible enough to adapt to any personally directed action research that might be designed:

1. **Look**
   - Gather relevant information. (Gather data.)
   - Build a picture that describes the situation. (Define and describe.)

2. **Think**
   - Explore and analyze: "What is happening here?" (Analyze.)
   - Interpret and explain: "How and why are things the way they are?" (Theorize.)

3. **Act**
   - Plan. (Outline and order.)
   - Implement and evaluate. (Act and report.)

His definitions (and our own) also imply processes that demand participation and negotiation from the people whose lives involve schools. In other words, you are not working alone on your research; you must consider the needs and desires of your colleagues and stakeholders. Such a research position (and there is no contradiction here) calls for both flexibility and rigorous work.

This step-by-step process might be deceptively linear in its appearance, but recall its spiralling nature. For Stringer, action research is an interacting, re-cycling spiral, within which the researcher is constantly looking back and considering what has already been done. This reflection informs and generates new actions.

Gummesson (2000) adds a second spiral to this research cycle: new understandings are developed and reconsidered naturally as new information comes to light. The process is iterative: in other words, each stage of work becomes part of action research.

To explain it differently, we always begin new research with pre-understandings about what the research is about. Think about it: you could not have chosen a subject you had absolutely no knowledge of. So accept that you started your research at a place of knowledge and experience. As your research progresses, it makes sense that you will learn more about it. In fact, the act of doing research takes on its own process and levels of understanding. Each level differs from the previous level, yet is built from knowledge gained in earlier activities.

In action research, you always venture into the unknown. You simply cannot control and understand everything that will happen. As you work, be rigorous, wise, and ethical. But—like in the 1989 Steven Spielberg movie *Indiana Jones and the Last Crusade* when Harrison Ford steps out over the abyss into what seems like nothingness—sometimes you just "gotta go for it."

ACTION RESEARCH MODEL 2: JEFFREY GLANZ

In his book *Action Research: An Educational Leader's Guide to School Improvement,* Jeffrey Glanz (1998, p. 85) describes a four-step process for action research:

1. **Select a focus.** For Glanz, selecting a focus includes:
   - deciding what you want to investigate
   - developing a series of questions about the area you've chosen
   - establishing a plan to answer the question

   As you focus on a problem, pose questions that will guide your research. Developing a series of guiding questions eventually leads to the specific research questions that organize your study. Selecting a focus also includes developing an initial research methodology. At this stage, the research methodology may simply include a simple series of what-to-do steps.

2. **Collect your data.** Once you have developed a workable research focus that attends to the improvement of an educational problem (or an opportunity to gain more knowledge), it is time to begin collecting data. As you work, use a variety of data-collection methods. Data-collection methods may include tests, surveys, interviews, or the examination of relevant documents.

   Immerse yourself in the work. Remember, any data you collect must be transformed into a usable form. The best definition of "usable" is a form that both (1) tells you what you need to know and (2) allows you to clearly explain the information to others in your final report.

3. **Analyze and interpret your findings.** Once relevant data have been collected, begin to analyze and interpret what you have. What do your data mean? What opportunities to act emerge from what you have learned? Your goal here is to represent your findings in a clear and meaningful manner for others, and to generate feasible next steps for the organization you are studying.

4. **Take action based on your findings.** The purpose of your site-based action research is to actually implement possible

interventions. Glanz notes that it is important to ground your recommendations and planned interventions in your data. In simple words, you need to show that your decisions followed logically from your findings. You didn't make your findings up; so, you can point to what finding led you to act. Were you not to use or trust your findings, there would be no reason to conduct research. Your decisions would be based on trial and error—and unconsidered trial and error at that.

Most action researchers note three possible choices you can make as you evaluate the actions (interventions) based on your research. These are obvious, though people seldom choose the second option: (1) continue the intervention, (2) call it off (disband the intervention), or (3) modify the intervention in ways that make sense, based on what you have learned.

Key first steps for planning action research

The action research models above, though somewhat different, both begin by attempting to understand the problem at hand. You should begin with this step as well. This early focus is important: without it, your research can grow into a huge quagmire of unconnected data. Care and attention in defining your research question at the early stage makes it easier in later stages when you want to organize your data into something that tells the "story" of an educational problem and its possible resolutions.

Defining your research question

It is possible in the early stages that you are unclear about what exactly you want to study. Some educators enter research with a clear sense of what interests them, but many are uncertain at the outset. Your comfort level might depend on how much research you have done. If you are new to organizing research tasks, do not be discouraged: the exercise of conducting research will build confidence more than you can imagine. If you do your research well, you will gain experience and knowledge. We can almost guarantee that you will see schools and your work in them with new, critical eyes. This growth is exciting.

One strategy for defining a research topic is to brainstorm, both alone and with colleagues—the idea here is to "play around." Another strategy is to keep a day-by-day journal of your work, and review it after a couple of weeks to see what themes emerge. You could also "free write" of a list of questions (no editing allowed). Try sketching diagrams or graphic representations of your thoughts. Read a book about work, or surf the Internet. Play in a database: key in search terms just to see what pops up.

Stay loose and open—the ideas will come if you play consciously. This "play" is important and uses skills you will need in later stages of the action research process. For example, once you have collected some data (inclusive of anything and everything you can examine—surveys, academic achievement, observations, etc.), you can use these skills to look for trends and adjust your research plan: What does your data tell you where your focus should be?

Central questions versus subquestions

Your **central research question** is the general question you wish to answer with a definite yes or no. For example:

- "Does assessment for learning help promote student achievement?"

Research subquestions are the specific questions you use to answer the central question. You can formulate research subquestions by restating your central question in a more open-ended way with different variables. For example:

- "To what extent (or to what degree) does assessment for learning impact (or influence) student engagement? Student comprehension? Student-teacher communication?"

Remember that you can, and probably will, adjust your central question and subquestions as you get your research underway. Your research is a learning process, and your central question and subquestions are works in progress.

And you are a work in progress, too. We like to say that there are two projects in every research project: learning something useful about what is being studied, and the growth of the researcher doing the study.

Other things to think through early

Research is an iterative process. You begin with a plan: you think things through as far and as well as you can. As you engage in the research itself—and you learn things—you think things through some more. With each iteration, you adjust your research plan and you add detail.

Here are some questions that we, as researchers, have found helpful early on:

- What am I going to research? What are my research questions?
  - What is my central question?
  - What subquestions must I ask and answer to answer my central question?

- What overall approach will guide me?
    - Am I curious (do I want to find information, truth, or fact)?
    - Do I want to make changes to a practice or an institution?
    - What is the overall function of my research?

- What will I consider as data?
    - Where will my data come from?
    - What will my data look like?
    - How can I organize these data well?

- What data-collection methods will I use?
    - What methodology generally fits my research questions?
    - How will I collect data?
    - What is feasible given time, monetary, and logistical constraints?
    - How can I work effectively and efficiently?
    - How can I work ethically?

- How will I evaluate my own research?
    - How do I, as a researcher, impact the research?
    - How will I know if my data are accurate?
    - How will I know if my data are useful?
    - What ethical considerations must I attend to?
    - What is my relationship to the research and those I involve in my research?
    - How can I limit my intrusion into the lives of others? (How can I be as psychologically and physically neat and considerate as possible?)

About organizational culture

Often research can shed light on unseen and seldom deconstructed contexts. Cultures exist and operate within all organizations, including schools, and many aspects are not readily apparent. If you consider your own experiences of becoming accustomed to the schools where you've worked, you will probably realize that some lessons learned were not in your school handbook. Those lessons included discovering where the rules were flexible and where they weren't, whether a school was open to new ideas, which departments were "happy" places and which were not, and who would bring doughnuts for Wednesday morning coffee. We call this getting a feel for an organization. An insider's perspective, developed over time, embodies aspects of organizational culture not obvious to outsiders.

On the other hand, an organization's insiders have their own blind spots. If your research focuses on your own organization, there may be aspects of its culture you have never questioned or studied. Perhaps you will not realize these nuances—in some cases hazard zones—until you trespass on someone's space.

Here's an example: Edna completed a site-based research project within her school district. Her report was comprehensive and complete. However, her superintendent—who had worked in the district for years—believed the report should follow a traditional, quantitative reporting format and style. He said, "That's the way we do it in education. If you don't write it this way, we won't take it seriously. In fact, we won't even read it." Edna considered her superintendent's point and decided to tailor her final report to the specific audience for whom she was writing.

If you are in a particular culture, you might already know people who—either through personal hardwiring or their own educational experience—will likely find your site-based action research too qualitative for their tastes. If they believe in standardized procedures and research neutrality, they may think you should do research in a particular way. They may be bothered that action research is often written in the first person or as a story. If you find yourself working with someone more in tune with quantitative research and reporting styles, what do you do? The answer is that, in the tradition of action research, you negotiate your decisions with that person.

In some educational settings, once you have obtained approval for your research, you will face few restrictions. In other settings, even if you receive official approval, someone may place demands on your reporting, limit your access to people or documents during your data collection, or request modifications to your work. That's the way culture works and, while it can be frustrating to make such adjustments, ultimately your work will not be useful unless it matches existing organizational values.

Case study: a teacher leader considers context

A social studies department head in a suburban high school had been struggling for a year to implement collaborative practices among her colleagues. Her predecessor, now retired, had implemented a "community of practice" model that asked staff to develop and act on a core mission statement. Scheduling had been adjusted to provide the staff with more time to work together. Yet meetings had broken down. Three teachers had developed a good collaborative working relationship as a result of the regular meeting times and taken full advantage of the opportunities these presented, but the rest of the department staff had drifted away from the process or were downright hostile to it.

Why had this department's collaborative efforts failed to gel when the math department, which had used the same collaborative model, was now a thriving team? Both departments were struggling with large classes and increasingly diverse student populations. Both departments had the same resources and number of staff. But as the new department head investigated the problem further, she discovered a number of contextual factors that distinguished the two departments:

- The math department staff was considerably younger and more open to change.
- Some teachers in the social studies department were still trying to adapt to major curriculum changes that had been brought in three years ago.
- The nonsupporters in her own department appeared to gather around a ringleader of sorts. This individual had personality conflicts with the former department head and had never engaged in collaborative efforts. Also he was (or so she believed) a good old boy who did not take her leadership seriously.
- Staff in social studies felt burdened by marking requirements, and noted that social studies and English language arts posed greater problems for senior high students with weak English language skills.

To begin to address the problem in her area, this social studies department head needed to ask questions, think carefully, and identify factors like those above that made her own department's challenge of implementing collaborative practices distinct from that of the math department. Each department, provided with the same resources and situated within the same larger context of the school, operated within unique contexts shaped by the demands of differing subject areas, and the histories and personalities of the staff involved.

Make the work workable

Doing research well does not take genius, but it does take thoughtful consideration. Action research does not rely on complex experiments or inferential statistics to extract meaning from data. The plans and decisions that shape site-based action research are practical and ethical; they stress common sense, consideration for others, and attention to detail.

To new or nonresearchers, research may seem difficult, esoteric, and confusing. The best researchers, though, do things as straightforwardly as possible.

Think as simply as possible: if you want to know the answer to a question, ask the question.

It's also useful to keep in mind that good site-based action research always includes the stages of negotiation, reflection, and implementation—sometimes in no particular order. The purpose of action research is to address a problem or question in a workable manner.

4

Completing a literature review

ESSENTIAL QUESTIONS

What is the purpose of a literature review when engaging in research?

What are the steps to conducting and writing an effective literature review?

CHAPTER PURPOSE

To introduce literature reviews and suggest manageable ways for teacher researchers to conduct them

To celebrate opportunities to enter into a conversation with other researchers who share interests similar to your own research agenda

In the last chapter, we talked about starting a research plan: framing your initial research questions and thinking things through as far as you can. We also talked about the iterative nature of research. A literature review is your first opportunity to learn more about what you want to do, and adjust your plan. It is also something that you will want to write up: at the end of your task, you will need to tell the story of what you did as an action researcher, what you learned, and what your findings produced. A literature review is an essential part of the story—and a very interesting part.

Literature reviews as conversations

If you really care about your research, you will want to talk to others about it. In many ways, doing a literature review is like conversing with others who care about the same things you do. The authors of the relevant research literature have chosen to invest their time and energies in the same area that you are investigating. As a result, you already have much in common. If you think about a literature review as talking to people who share similar interests, a literature review is something to enjoy.

attitude

Sadly, many new researchers see a literature review as a chore—something that must be done before they can begin to work. They do it dutifully rather than with a celebratory spirit. Such lack of enthusiasm is unfortunate, and researchers who engage literature reviews in this spirit miss the encouragement and advice others in the research community might offer about the two most important things in their research: (1) content and (2) method.

Reading the work of others in your area of interest is like talking over what has been discovered (content) and how discoveries have been made and articulated (method). These insights will help you plan and conduct your own site-based action research.

Reading with an open mind

You have time to get your research questions

Many research books will tell you: first, nail down your research questions; next, conduct a research (literature) review. This approach does not reflect how real researchers work. Real researchers are never _not_ working on their review of literature; they are *always* reading in their areas of interest. Their reading and research meld together. The steps of defining research questions and reviewing the literature happen at the same time. In action research, these steps are part of the spiral process of reflection-action-evaluation described in the last chapter.

We believe you only need a germ of an idea to begin working on your literature review. In fact, if your idea is too concrete—if you are stuck in it—you are not open to what you read and the literature won't speak to you. Conversely, if you remain flexible about your own ideas and engage the literature with an open mind, your reading actually shapes your thinking. It is never too early to begin your literature review—a sort of turning over of rocks and allowing the ideas beneath to spring to life. In the step-by-step process that follows, this sense of natural development is implicit in the process. If you review literature well, your review will add to your project.

Reflecting on your research with others

As you complete any step of your task, there is no reason not to share your ideas with researchers whose work you have consulted, given these days of easy, instant access to others through e-mail and online social networks. Our world is shrinking and that is reflected in the contracted "distance" between established and emerging researchers. Many researchers are willing to and can really help—regardless of how famous they might be. One of Jim's students took the challenge and sent her work to well-known media and culture critic Neil Postman. Not only did Postman respond personally to her ideas, he encouraged her to visit him to talk further!

Your literature review allows you to gain a better understanding of your research task. In all likelihood, it will also begin to reveal possible insights into the central question that interests you. That's the way it works. Conversing with the literature enables a researcher to draw on and share existing knowledge and expertise in an area of interest. Literature reviews are collaborations of perspectives, and it is important that you take yourself seriously in this collaboration: your thoughts and observations are valuable contributions to the research community.

Synthesizing what you read

A literature review is more than a compilation of findings. It is an evaluation of what other scholars and researchers have written about your area of interest. It is entirely focused on the problem or issue you wish to address and how you will address it. Take ownership of what you learn. To do this work well, you must learn to recognize relevant information, synthesize it, and evaluate its worth for your study.

For example, did you notice a few paragraphs back that we commented on what most research books tell you about doing a literature review? We *criticized* the notion of beginning your review after choosing your question as failing to understand how real researchers work. What gives us the right to be critical about these books? We've put in our time as researchers and, when you research as a vocation, you develop confident insights. You will develop the same confidence and fluency in your own area of interest as you gain experience by consulting and wrestling with the literature.

Some useful insights from others on literature reviews

Here are some thoughts from other seasoned researchers on the value and nature of literature reviews.

Why a literature review is important

The Alberta Teachers' Association (2000, p. 20) makes these points:

It creates a permanent record for future reference.

It helps build continuity for the project if the participants change.

It is a valuable part of sharing your work with others.

It can be used to support further research, including applications for funding for you or others.

What a good literature review requires
Taylor (2001) identifies the following processes as crucial:
- information seeking—the ability to efficiently scan the literature using manual or computerized search methods to identify potentially useful articles and books
- critical appraisal—the ability to apply principles of analysis to identify studies that are unbiased and valid
- organized presentation—the ability to organize literature into meaningful constructs

What to ask while reading the literature
Bogdan and Biklen (1992, p. 169) suggest these questions:

What crucial issues are noted in the literature?

What past findings have a bearing on your setting?

How does your perspective differ from those you have read? How does it agree?

What has been neglected in the literature?

Reading literature critically
In 1996, physicist Alan Sokal undertook what he called "a modest (though admittedly uncontrolled) experiment" (as quoted in Spiller, 2004, p. 181). He wondered if a leading North American journal of cultural studies would publish a nonsense article if it sounded good and flattered the editors' preconceptions. Sokal submitted a nonsense article entitled "Transgressing the Boundaries: Toward a Transformative Hermeneutics of Quantum Gravity" to the prestigious academic journal *Social Text* and, though his work was fabricated and nonsensical, it was published in the journal's spring/summer 1996 issue. Simultaneously, Sokal admitted his prank in another journal. The result was a laugh for those who tend to believe—as we do—that published work can be aggressively esoteric. His success amounted to egg on the face of the editors at *Social Text,* and caused a small uproar in the rest of the academic world—only some of it laughter.

Although Sokal's actions were perhaps ethically questionable, he challenged what he felt was substandard—yet widely read and published—academic work. His defenders compared him to the child in *The Emperor's New Clothes,* who dared to use common sense to point out the obvious.

Our purpose in relating this tale is to encourage you to use your own common sense when something you read strikes you as "off the mark." Certainly we do not suggest that the authenticity of all academic work can be challenged; generally, academic work is produced by serious people whose goals are similar to our own. Most academic work is completed (and reviewed by others) carefully and responsibly. However, writers and reviewers have their own perspectives, judgments, and blind spots. We call these *biases* in our book. Whatever you call them, everyone comes to dinner with a favourite food.

Such biases can leave new researchers with a problem. How do you recognize what's valuable? Your challenge is to find valid literature to help you to make decisions and better understand the areas you have chosen to research. A first step, when reading research for a literature review is to spot "where authors are coming from" by using your critical thinking skills and your own common sense.

Of course, critical reading involves more than simply pronouncing a written work good or bad. Fenwick and Parsons (2009) believe the point is not to tear apart the literature, but to think of contributions to the literature as partial perspectives (there are two—or more—sides to every story) from particular communities, infused with the desires and assumptions of specific authors, cultures, times, and places. Your job, when reading, is (1) to determine what perspective is offered by a particular work and (2) to consider how that perspective applies to your own research.

Considering context

First, what is the context of the article? By this we mean, where did the article come from and why was it written? In the same way newspapers can lean left or right in political orientation, articles related to your research can be shaped by ideologies. In their own ways, educational journals have constituencies. Some are written for human resources staff; some are written for psychologists; some are written for Marxists; some for administrators. When you read, it is wise to know where authors are coming from and where they are going. For instance, from the examples above, how would the viewpoints of a Marxist translate for a typical Fortune 500 CEO in the United States? And these are not the only mixes and matches you might find.

We can also think of differences in *historical* context. For example, we once worked on a Canadian-based broadband cable study that partnered our university with another university. For whatever reason, in an attempt to make the work easier or to rely on already established external validity measures, the partner university insisted on using a then four-year-old survey instrument that was piloted in, and designed for, the southern United States. Does your critical reading of this situation get your antennae twitching as it did ours? The United States—especially the southern United States—differs from Canada in important ways, such as demography, social structure, and education. In addition, four years is a lot when studying technology.

Our critical reading suggested that this survey instrument would not produce valid findings for our study.

Some research articles can become dated—or perhaps not? Although most of your reading will probably be quite current, you might want to consider older articles. You need to approach older articles with some sensitivity to thoughts and ideas current for the time they were written. For instance, you've no doubt encountered the ubiquitous term *life-long learning*. This term generally fits a notion of adult education as something centred in work environments, whose aim is to advance organizations and individual careers. However, if you were to study articles from the 1960s and 1970s in the area of adult education, you would find a left-to-radical conception of adult learning. Specifically, adult education was often conceived as a democratic undertaking that would help ordinary people use knowledge to challenge social injustices.

Finally, it is important to consider how organizations might be affiliated with the literature you are reading. Who does the author "work for"? Who sponsored the research you are reading? How does funding impact a study? For example, publications emerging from well-funded projects often differ from projects with obvious funding issues. Some projects carry with them the interest of presenting work positively to the public, others to show structural inequities within a system.

To persuade or to inform?

Some information is simple to grasp. Jim asks Kurtis what he did yesterday. Kurtis replies: "I made revisions to an article I have been working on." This response answers Jim's question "What did you do?" with a straightforward answer. The answer is *factual*. Quantitatively, Jim could ask Kurtis the same question each day and collect his answers over a time period—over a year, for example. Jim would then know what Kurtis did over that time period.

However, most research is more complex than adding up daily answers. Because we are dealing with qualitative research and because most action research deals with human behaviour, you'll encounter few examples of straightforward answers. Remember, human beings are quirky and diverse. There are few hard-and-fast rules about the ways we should organize ourselves and interact with one another.

You won't find many straightforward presentations of facts in research articles, either. Rather, most of what you read will be an attempt to *persuade* you to agree with the author's beliefs on a given topic. Your job as a critical reader is to look beyond what the person is saying to ask the more difficult questions about whether what is being said is reasonable and convincing, and what the arguments presented mean for your research.

Entire volumes are written about the art and science of critical thinking. Our goal here is simply to raise your awareness of occasions when you might be reading with *uncritical* acceptance (we all do sometimes). To keep a critical eye, ask a few simple questions:

- What argument is being presented?
- What persuasive techniques does the author use to encourage you to buy into her argument? How valid is the argument presented?
- Are these techniques fair play? Do you believe the argument is fair and reasonable? Is it clear that the author understands the argument?
- Finally, how does this argument apply to your work?

Let us give you a quick example of how to be critical—yet not dismissive—of a piece of academic writing. Peter Vaill's (1996) *Learning as a Way of Being: Strategies for Survival in a World of Permanent White Water* is considered, in some circles, a classic. To be accurate, he makes excellent points about the nature of organizational life. We say this because we don't want you to believe we are simply dumping on his ideas. However, Vaill uses the phrase "permanent white water" (p. 4) in an almost uncritical way. More to the point, some readers we have worked with seem to *trot out this phrase* (notice our use of italics to describe this—that is a hint) to note general acceptance of a condition they believe explains the nature of life within organizations. They then leave it as "the truth," like an egg delivered by the Easter Bunny.

But let us lead you through the way we, as practising researchers, critically consider this language. First, we really don't think organizational life is "permanent white water"; the phrase is more a "colourful" than accurate reflection of organizational complexities. For example, we honestly believe some aspects of organizational culture do *not* change, nor should they. We believe good relationships always make better working spaces. We believe honest concern for others—even *clients*—is persuasive. We believe that organizations—even universities—that offer good programs do better than those who are slick but lack substance. And so on. Second, if we did believe life was permanent white water, what are the implications of holding this belief? Should we lose hope because change is impossible? Is there no rock upon which to build an organizational home? Are we driven to a state of permanent ennui because we cannot deal with the ramifications of such turmoil and confusion?

Our point is, when you think about this phrase, there are just times when it doesn't work. Therefore, although we value Vaill's insights, we cannot accept everything he says as completely true.

The ancient roots of the art of persuasion

If you think persuasion is a new concept, you may be surprised to hear that the ancient Greeks, who were so interested in language, systematically studied the "art" of persuasion. In fact, the ever-categorizing Aristotle identified three distinct types of persuasion:

Ethical (ethos): this technique links the persuasive goal to an ethic so powerful or unquestioned that few would think to challenge the claim. This persuasion style often rests on the credibility of the issue or the presenter. For example, if Angelina Jolie supports a cause or a product, perhaps you should as well.

Pathetic (pathos): this technique links the persuasive goal to an emotionally attractive outcome that is so good for you that you feel compelled to follow its directives. For example, fathers might tell us, "Once you get your education, the world will open up before you." Or, spam e-mail suggests that a certain diet or a stomach staple will help you lose 40 pounds in three days.

Logical (logos): in this case, the technique links the persuasive goal to a societal or cultural understanding so ingrained that the goal is hard to resist. For example, a company that sells toilet tissue tells you that their product is the softest money can buy. They are appealing to an understanding in our society that "soft toilet paper is better than scratchy toilet paper"—and can we disagree?

Research literature, although much deeper and more educational than most advertisements, must be carefully considered before you buy into it. You must always ask: "What are they selling and how are they selling it?"

Privileged views and voices

Do you know Buddha's story of the seven blind men and the elephant? Each blind man encounters only one part of the elephant—a leg, the trunk, an ear—so each has a very different idea of what an elephant is like. A "research elephant," of course, is like the truth, and we are all somewhat blind in that we cannot perceive that whole truth; we need the voices and perspectives of others.

There are two implications here. The first is to acknowledge your own blind spots. No doubt you bring your own ideas and beliefs to your reading. For some the temptation is to read and seriously consider only what *confirms* their biases. Don't we all wish to live in echo chambers where we are right and where people agree with us? Unfortunately, this approach can leave us right about only one part of the elephant, with a weak understanding of the whole animal. In short, a literature review should be a wide and careful reading that also helps you thoughtfully consider what you *don't* agree with.

The second implication is that the authors you read are in exactly the same boat. They too have biases; they too make choices about whether they will explore (or openly reveal) those biases in their work. In other words, an author might not see the whole elephant either. Here is another excellent reason to cast a wide research-literature net. By comparing much work, you develop a stronger sense of where an individual author's biases might lie.

When we speak of "privileging" certain perspectives, we mean that any work—including your own—might be critically examined for the views, beliefs, and biases of people whose interests receive the most attention. Our work as researchers, and as critical readers, is to recognize privileged perspectives and to strive for the bigger picture.

Somewhere between blind acceptance and paranoia

In our own experience as research mentors, we've seen extremes of both blind acceptance and paranoia. Some people take most everything they read as gospel, often because they feel they lack expertise to challenge what they read. (This feeling, by the way, is false. If you do not have the expertise to be critical of what you read, drop the idea that you can do research right now!) Others get so carried away with their critical-thinking superpower that they criticize (rather than critique) everything they read and look for hidden agendas everywhere. Most of us muddle about somewhere in the middle, remaining open to ideas we encounter while developing confidence to challenge and question these ideas when something doesn't sit right. It's a careful balance, but one achieved by reading widely and sharing your own thoughts, ideas, and responses with critical friends. Today's networked world allows us more easily than ever to share our developing thoughts and theories with a global community, through blogs and social networks.

Questions for critical reading

The following questions may help you to carefully consider what you read, and use your own experience, common sense, and critical-thinking skills to assess merit. Remember, not all academic literature is created equally.

Purpose

Why was this text written?
What purpose do you think it serves?
What audience does it address?

Historical context

When was the article written?

Does it reflect the thinking or trends of a given era?

Authorship

Who is the author? What biases or perspectives might the author bring to the work?

What is stated as "evident" in the article? How might the author's occupation, politics, or other affiliations shape her thinking?

Arguments

If the author takes a strong position on a topic, how does he represent others?

Are contrary perspectives addressed? Are they addressed fairly?

Are issues pertaining to race, class, and/or gender fairly portrayed?

Does the author show sensitivity to different worldviews?

Steps in conducting a literature review

This section has two purposes. First, we want to help you look for research literature. Even if you have partially completed a review, this might lead you to new, useful articles. Second, even if you do not know the specific questions you will pursue, be confident that you can begin your review immediately—because, in doing the review, you will find your path. Frankly, it would be hard for us to imagine that anyone reading this paragraph would not have some idea of their research area of interest. It is time to start looking around generally and trusting that your "conversations" with the literature will guide you toward specificity.

If you are like other researchers, you have formulated some initial research questions but have not quite decided how you will conduct your research. That is, you have not finalized your research method or research plan. Soon, you will need to organize your plan. However, even if you have not taken this step, we believe you should begin to work on your literature review anyway. We trust this activity will help you clarify the research plan you will use to answer your research questions.

We know that you know the area of your study. Your task now is to use what you already know to seek information about what other researchers have found. Remember, these researchers already care about the same problems you do and have already done their work. You will use what they have learned to further your own understanding.

We believe a review of literature should be a community celebration. Relax and enjoy. We encourage you not to miss possibilities:

read thoroughly and don't rush. In fact, reading thoroughly in the first place actually saves you time in the long run. Some articles you read might not directly transfer into your finalized work; however, the process of reviewing the literature, and the information you discover, will help you to complete your work. Why repeat what someone else has already done?

Remember that in a literature review, you are working on two goals: (1) to discover literature that addresses your own area of interest and (2) to help you organize your research plan. For this activity, it doesn't matter which goal you are pursuing. All roads lead to Rome, as they say. As practising researchers, our process for conducting literature reviews goes generally like this:

- Conduct a search on the Internet using key terms.
- Ask others for suggestions of key researchers and literature (you could consult leaders in professional development for direction).
- Generate a collection of 25 to 30 articles to review.
- Read these articles and take notes.
- Organize the notes into an outline.
- Use the outline to write the literature review.

The process is straightforward, but it's also lengthy and involves practical matters such as *how* you identify key terms and collect 30 articles. What follows is a more step-by-step approach that has worked well for us. Don't become overwhelmed as you read through these steps the first time. It might seem like a lot at first, but if you follow the steps one at a time, things become clear.

Step 1: Make a map. If you have a general idea of the research method you want to use, begin by making a point-form outline or a concept map of what you already know. We start with concept maps or mind maps because they don't push *solutions* too quickly; they're kind of a mental warm-up. If you are able to complete this task easily, jump right to step 3. If this task was difficult and you're still confused about the specifics of what you want to research, go to step 2. In either case, don't worry—you can work from there.

Step 2: Start to work. If you are still deciding what (specifically) you want to research or you haven't decided on what approach you will take, there is no reason for concern. It doesn't mean that you can't or shouldn't start working. Just choose the initial (or general) area and approach that interests you. You will naturally narrow your focus as you read more.

Step 3: Organize in advance. If you are now fairly clear about your research area and method, the next step is to collect your information. Use online document storage or a flash drive, or create a folder on your hard drive. Consider which technique will be most easily accessible, and remember to create a periodic backup! Because you will use the Internet for this portion of your work, get in the habit of saving your work as you go. Saving as you go could potentially save you much time and grief later. Using the Internet might also mean creating word files complete with http addresses and the dates you accessed each site.

Step 4: Visit the library. If you are confused about where to search, visit your university library's website, which provides a number of online resources to help you. Better: if you can, go into the library and talk to a real flesh-and-blood librarian (they still exist). In our experience, resource-desk staff and librarians are "angels of the archives"; they know their stuff and want to help.

Step 5: Determine your keywords. When you have figured out which databases to search—we suggest starting with ERIC (Education Resources Information Center)—decide what keywords you will use to search. Here, a concept map can help. Notice the words you used to describe your research area, and begin searching with these words as key terms. Don't be discouraged if at first they don't work. You might need to play around and explore, because the English language is filled with synonyms. You might be onto something wonderful, but perhaps have not yet discovered the *language* of the topic.

Step 6: Be selective. Once you've found workable keywords, choose about 25 of the best, most relevant articles. Save these, and limit yourself to working through these before any more searching. Some people go crazy and begin to review everything, but such seduction might put you in over your head before you know it, and you can drown in information. We say: review only the number of articles you picked at the start.

Step 7: Read in brief. Scan the articles or read the abstracts to get the lay of the land. You are probably anxious to read, or you might see greater value in just diving into the whole text. However, from our experience, abstracts are valuable tools. They can save you time in these early stages, where your goal is to gain a general feel for your research area. Save your thorough reading for later in this process.

Step 8: Build your references. As you save and review your articles, take time to copy complete citation information on each of them. Get in the habit of keeping consistent bibliographical information from the start. Such rigour will save you time and aggravation in the long run.

Reading and taking notes

As you read and evaluate the literature, you need to carefully and systematically record what you find, both for your own work as a researcher and for those who follow. Others will read and consider your work, so you need to clearly document your path through the literature.

You can read and take notes one of two ways: digitally or on paper.

Digital note taking

Once you've scanned your articles, it is time to read more thoroughly and take notes. The process we outline below assumes you are reading and taking notes as you go. If you are a "print person" and prefer to work with hard copies of the literature, jump straight down to the next section about taking notes on paper, which gives instructions for reading and note taking the old-fashioned way. "Computer people," read on.

1. Open two documents on your computer. Name the first **reference list** and the second **notes**. (Some people call a *reference list* a *bibliography*, but we are following the protocols and terminology of the American Psychological Association.)
2. Now open the first article you've saved—say it's called "Organizational Theory.doc." Rename this document so the name begins with the number 1—now it's called "1 Organizational Theory. doc." We call the *1* the "article number." Save the article under the new name.
3. Copy the article's full citation, and paste one copy in your **reference list** document and one copy in your **notes** document. Include the article number with each citation. You have now created a cross-referencing system that will keep the article, its citation, and your notes on the article linked with the article number (see Figure 2).
4. In your **notes** document underneath the citation you've copied, begin to take notes on the first article as you read thoroughly. Cut and paste any direct quotes from the article you feel may be helpful. Be sure to record the page numbers as you do so.
5. Repeat the process with the second article you open and read, renaming it with a number 2 and copying its citation to your **reference list** and **notes**. Take your notes for the second article underneath its citation in your **notes** document.

Figure 2 DOCUMENT ORGANIZATION FOR TAKING NOTES ON COMPUTER

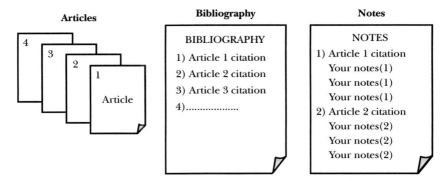

6. Continue this process with each article you read. Be sure to match the article number across documents each time. When you are finished, you should have a **reference list** that contains citations for the articles you read, numbered in the order you read them, and a fairly lengthy **notes** document that contains the citation and your notes for each article, again numbered in the order you read them.

7. Now turn your attention to the **notes** document you have created. Read your notes over on screen. As you read, do the following:
   - Add any brief personal comments or observations right into the text as you go. We say "brief" because you are still taking notes; we don't believe you should start to write yet, but we don't want you to miss ideas either.
   - When you have completed your reading, write a short phrase—just a few words—to summarize what each note is about. Try to categorize your notes using a set number of summary phrases (we recommend somewhere in the neighbourhood of four to seven topic headings). These categories will help you to sort the notes into usable themes or subsections for your literature review. If you don't know what to call a particular note, create a "miscellaneous" category for now.
   - At the beginning of each of your notes, type the article number to which it corresponds.

8. Now, open a new document in your computer called **sorted notes**. List the category phrases (headings) you used to classify your notes in the last step. These will serve as a rough outline for your literature review. Don't worry about the organization of these categories now. This is not *The Old Man and the Sea*; you are not writing a literary masterwork. Just choose an order for your

ENGAGING IN ACTION RESEARCH

categories and stick with it. The sections of the final document are easily moved around in entire blocks anyway, if you change your mind later.

9. Copy the first note in your **notes** document and paste it into its correct category in **sorted notes**.

10. Repeat this process with each set of notes. When you are finished, you will have sorted all your notes by the categories you've ascribed to them.

11. Print the document **sorted notes**.

12. The next step is to literally cut and paste the notes in each category into a logical order, remembering that the final order can be almost any logical structure. Working with one category or theme at a time, cut out your printed notes and use a glue stick to paste them in the correct (logical) order on another sheet of paper. Do the same for each category until the task is completed.

13. Return to your computer and reorganize each section of **sorted notes** on your screen by moving the notes into the cut-and-paste order that you created in the last step. (Remember not to lose the article number for each note as you work.) You have now created the first draft of your literature review.

14. Now you can begin to write, editing the notes into a smooth, readable format. Replace the article numbers in your notes with proper citations to the articles. Link the sections together with appropriate transitions. Plan to go through three or four quick revisions, so don't try to make all the changes the first time through. Just read and edit what gets your attention as you go. Add your own thoughts, evaluations, and critiques as you write and revise.

15. When you've done a number of revisions, you are ready to write a one- or two-paragraph introduction section and a one- or two-paragraph conclusion. These can say whatever you want, but an introduction usually: sets out the themes or titles to follow; lists the areas or types of journals (like "adult education" or "administration and leadership") where you found the best literature; and gives the reader a clue about what's coming. The conclusion basically summarizes the literature review and pulls three or four highlights from it.

16. Save your **reference list**. Remove the article numbers and sort your citations alphabetically. Be sure to review the reference list for conformity to APA (American Psychological Association) standards.

17. Congratulations! You're done the literature review section of your research.

Taking notes on paper

If you prefer to take notes on computer as we've described above, skip this section and go to the next section on converting notes to paragraphs. If you are a print person who processes things better using good old-fashioned written pages, read on. You will start your note-taking process with the stack of articles you have printed off to read. Make sure you have complete reference information for each article, preferably attached to the front of the article or at the top.

1. First, you may want to photocopy your articles. Later, you'll be messing them up with highlighters, notes, and scissors. You may want a "clean" copy of the articles in print form to refer back to later.
2. Call the first article you read "article 1." (Write this—we call it the "article number"—in large letters across the top of the article, or on the reference information you have attached to the front.)
3. Name a blank sheet of paper **categories**.
4. Begin reading your first article. When you come across something noteworthy, you'll need to:
   - Highlight it.
   - Write the article number in the margin beside the section you've highlighted. Also in the margin, write a one- or two-word category that the highlighted piece would fit into.
   - List each category on the **categories** sheet.

5. As you highlight new pieces, either assign them to an existing category or create new categories as needed, adding each new category to your **categories** sheet. Later, you will use these categories to organize your literature review into sections, so keep this in mind as you choose them. Ideally, you should have between four and seven categories to work from.
6. Name a separate sheet of paper **personal ideas**. As you read, record any thoughts or ideas that come to you. Be sure to label each note you make here with (a) the article number it pertains to, and (b) the category it would fit into.
7. Repeat this process with each article you read, numbering the articles as you go.
8. When you have finished reading and highlighting all of your articles, turn your attention to the **categories** sheet you created. Can you picture how these categories might be used to organize your literature review? Do you need to combine some categories to make the process more manageable? In what order, for now, do they make the most sense?

9. Now you will need a handful of large (preferably used or recycled) envelopes. Label the front of each envelope with a category. Label one additional envelope **citations**.

10. Return to the pile of articles you have read and highlighted. Cut out the pieces you highlighted, making sure that each includes your margin notes of (1) the article number the piece comes from and (2) the category it fits into. As you cut, put each piece into its corresponding category envelope. For each article, you should also cut out the reference information and put it in the **citations** envelope. Once you have finished cutting out the good stuff, the rest of your scraps can be tossed out.

11. You will need some workspace for the next step, plus a glue stick and some paper. (You can use recycled paper for this; you only need one "good" side to work on.) Take the first envelope and dump your cuttings on the table. Look them over, then glue them onto a sheet of paper in an order that makes sense to you. Remember, there are many ways to order the information—you are not creating a masterpiece. The point is, don't worry too much. You can make changes later if you need to. Remember to number the sheets so you can review them in the correct order. Return these sheets to the envelope.

12. Repeat this process with each of the envelopes and categories.

13. Turn to your **citations** envelope. Glue the individual citations onto a piece of paper in the order of their article numbers (the order in which you initially read the articles). You will use this sheet to help you write the draft of your literature review. Figure 3 shows what you should have in front of you by now.

14. Now you are ready to convert your notes into a readable format. It is important right now that you don't try to do too much—remember, one step at a time! Key your cut-and-paste notes from each category envelope into the computer. Referring to your **citations** sheet, replace the article numbers in the notes with proper references. You may add any other notes as they come to you, but don't let this slow you down. Work as quickly as possible and don't worry too much about editing right now—you can do that later.

15. Now you can begin to write, editing the notes into a smooth, readable format. Link the sections together with appropriate transitions. Plan to go through three or four quick revisions, so don't try to make every change the first time through. Just read and edit what gets your attention as you go. Refer to your sheet of **personal ideas** to add your own thoughts, evaluations, and critiques as you write and revise.

Figure 3 DOCUMENT ORGANIZATION FOR TAKING NOTES ON PAPER

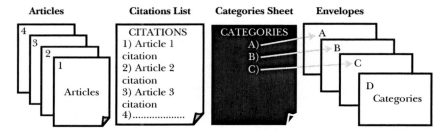

16. When you've done a number of revisions, you are ready to write a one- or two-paragraph introduction section and a one- or two-paragraph conclusion. These can say whatever you want, but an introduction usually: sets out the themes or titles to follow; lists the areas or types of journals (like "adult education" or "administration and leadership") where you found the best literature; and gives the reader a clue about what's coming. The conclusion basically summarizes the literature review and pulls three or four highlights from it.

17. Use your cut-and-paste page of **citations** to write your reference list. Be sure to review the reference list for conformity to APA (American Psychological Association) standards.

18. Congratulations! You're done the literature review section of your project.

Converting notes to paragraphs: an example

For those new to writing literature reviews, this section presents a paragraph as a model for writing. Note that the author and the year usually come first in the sentence, followed by what the author found. Consult an appropriate style guide for more advice on including references in your text. Most social sciences use APA style. You can buy the book (there is always a new edition), but you may very well be able to get by on the many, many "unofficial" style guides online. Use the keywords *APA style* in your search engine to locate these. We suggest the APA-inspired guidelines from the Purdue Online Writing Lab (Purdue University).

As you write, offer some critical commentary if you can. Try to engage the work and mould it to the needs of your own research rather than just listing off what you've found like so many numbers in a phone book. Writing a literature review is much like repeating a group discussion that you had with several people, and it can be written as such.

Writing literature reviews is quite formulaic. It's simply a matter of listing your review findings in a logical fashion and mixing up your verbs a little to make your writing more interesting. Try not to repeat the same verb over and over again: *said, said, said.* We suggest using different verbs, although this practice is not absolutely necessary. Try verbs such as (in no particular order): *observes, challenges, states, believes, cautions, warns, agrees, explains, reiterates, echoes, finds, concurs, suggests,* or *proposes.*

Here's an example of converting raw notes into a paragraph for a literature review. First, the raw notes.

Notes category: mentoring

(Article 2) Not appropriate for organizations that prefer control and predictable outcomes (Bowen 2004)

(Article 7) Weakness of mentoring—leaders need advanced agendas, grasp of potential outcomes or goes nowhere (Edison, 2006)

- Better if agenda determined by participants, but they have to be committed
- Mentorship holistic, nonlinear

(Article 3) Sand & Bowen (2009). Mentoring successful when: clear purpose, high commitment by participants, leaders to work both w. process and its outcomes

(Article 12) Huckle (2004). "this technique works best in situations characterized by uncertainty, ambiguity, and a recognition that new ideas are needed." (2004, p. 4)

(Article 6) Sweet (2011, p. 129). "the participants must volunteer and will reorganize based on personal interest and individual ability."

After looking at these notes, your task is to "write through" the raw notes, making sense and keeping it conversational as you go.

Bowen (2004) cautions organizations that prefer control and predictable outcomes not to consider mentoring. Edison (2006) believes the weakness of mentoring is the lack of control by leaders who attempt to work without advanced agendas or notions about potential outcomes. Since the participants determine the agenda, people must take responsibility, be open, and work in a process that is holistic, not linear. Furthermore, expert facilitation is required. According to Sand and Bowen (2009), the most successful mentoring occurs when the purpose is clear and there is a high commitment from participants and senior leaders to honour the outcome and process. Huckle (2004) observes, through his experience with Bowen's approach, "this technique works best in situations characterized by uncertainty, ambiguity, and a recognition that new ideas are needed" (p. 4). Sweet (2011) agrees that "participants must volunteer and they will reorganize based on personal interest and individual ability" (p. 129).

Draft your literature review early

We have said that you don't need to finalize your research questions or method before you begin your literature review. We encourage you, however, to complete a serious draft of your literature review before you begin to collect your data.

A serious draft is not a finished draft—it doesn't mean you are "done" reading the research literature. Every once in a while, you will need to take a vacation from your research without actually stopping the work. These little "vacations" are good times to take a new look at the literature (with fresh eyes that come from experience). Add whatever you find into your literature review when you find it. In this way, your literature review stays up to date. Don't fall victim to the plight of those who complete their research project and then find they have lost track of current research in their area.

Ready to go exploring

If you approach your literature review as an extensive study of volumes of peer-reviewed articles, accomplished through endless nights in the library surrounded by a makeshift fort of books, it is likely going to seem insurmountable. If you approach it as a chance to explore what others have said or found out about your research topic, it can become an ongoing activity that is deeply connected to your research. Often, the process of a literature review can be filled with excitement and reward, as you engage in conversations related to your work and research interests.

Capitalize on the experiences of those who have come before you. What have they found out that can inform your research? What knowledge do they share that can expand your own understanding of the question you're attempting to answer? Engaging in a literature review can be an incredibly gratifying activity, as you discover the uncharted water that your own research is attempting to navigate. Your literature review is the map that shows where others have come before you—your research is now setting forth to fill in the unknown.

5

Designing your research method

What is a research plan?

What are key data-collection methods?

What are the steps for formulating and writing an effective research plan?

CHAPTER PURPOSE

To introduce key data-collection methods

To suggest ways to structure research plans into a workable, step-by-step process for teacher researchers

Once you have figured out the questions you want to ask through your research, the next step is figuring out how you will answer them. If you have done your work well, you have made decisions that stem from your interests (including your organization's needs) and from reading what others interested in your research area have done. This background thinking and your literature review are complete—for now, more or less—and you are ready to design your research method, the step-by-step plan that will lead to the information you want.

The point of a research method or plan is to: (1) provide an organized structure for collecting the data you need, and (2) provide those who read your work with insight into what you did to find what you wanted to know.

One attractive feature of site-based action research is that it is more a research philosophy than a hard-and-fast rule book. This means that it can be completed using a wide variety of strategies. In site-based action research, the problem or challenge under investigation is often negotiated between the researcher and the researched, and the strategies for conducting the investigation can be negotiated as well. Action researchers choose (or construct) specific strategies that have the best chance of actually working—of doing the task they and their research participants hope it will do.

In this section, we review (in a nuts-and-bolts way) some key research strategies—activities you can use to collect data. Perhaps more importantly, we offer advice about structuring these activities into a workable, step-by-step process. As so often seems to be the case, effort expended in planning saves lots of grief later.

Ways to find out what you want to know

When collecting data about research subjects, there really are only a few ways to go at it. Todd Jick's (1979) important and classic research article "Mixing Qualitative and Quantitative Methods: Triangulation in Action" suggests how very simple collecting data can be. Jick says there are basically only four ways to find out about research subjects (p. 605):

- Ask research participants directly (use interviews, questionnaires, and self-reports).
- Ask research participants indirectly (use psychological instruments or projective tests—Myers-Briggs is one you might know).
- Ask those who interact with research participants (ask coworkers about their observations or perceptions).
- Observe participants' actions or past actions (observe and/or analyze relevant documents, text, or context).

Of course there are many subcategories, and each strategy itself could be the basis of an entire book on data-collection methods. Volumes, for example, have been written about observation strategies from the early anthropology of Margaret Mead to participant-observation studies where the researcher joins in with the activities of the group she is studying. Some great examples of participant observation include the studies by Marsh, Rosser, and Harre (1978) of football hooligans and Corsaro (1985) of children's friendships.

However, good research is mostly just common sense and can be done well by any careful and attentive researcher. Typical site-based action research projects use combinations of quantitative and qualitative approaches that often include interviews, focus groups, surveys, observation, and document analysis.

Interviews

Most data-collection methods are not all that difficult—hardly rocket science. And among all data-collection methods, interviews may be the most straightforward. Basically, the researcher figures out what he wants to know and asks the person he believes knows.

For example, last year a teacher wanted to know how new teachers worked, so she found and contacted a small number of new teachers and spoke with them about their work. To gain similar information from these new teachers, whose insights were the focus of her inquiry, she conducted a "structured interview." This means that she set out a series of specific questions she desired answers to and asked each new teacher she interviewed the same questions. Her data-collection instrument was a printout of a small number of questions, and she asked each and every interviewee each question in a systematic and precise fashion. Her conversations might have differed, as you would expect from human to human, but she was careful to ask and write down answers to each question.

Such a structured interview uses a short instrument to gather data face to face or, sometimes, over the telephone or by digital means. Such an instrument might be on a computer, instead of a piece of paper, and the interviewer might record responses digitally as well.

Because interviews take time and require transcription later (although some recent researchers have had great success with court reporter–type stenographers who provide an immediate transcription at the end of a session, with little difference in cost), a researcher needs to compare the benefits of different types of data-collection methods. It might, for example, be easier and cheaper—and as rich in responses—to simply use questionnaires to survey participants' insights. Researchers must consider the "bang for the buck" ratio—in terms of finances, time, and energy—in choosing one data-collection method over another. We believe simple is generally better than complex.

When creating a set of structured interview questions, the researcher must first create a broad set of questions that participants should answer. Second, the researcher should organize broad goals into a smaller, finite number of questions. Often, novice researchers create huge lists of questions, when a few questions would do just as nicely. They forget one maxim that we believe wholeheartedly: "Every person's favourite topic is himself/herself." This is not a cynical comment, simply recognition that one question and the ensuing conversation can uncover a whole world of insight.

Researchers use interviews to allow participants to share their situations, and to give each person a voice and opportunity to be heard.

Because research must be done ethically, a researcher should always seek permission to ask questions and to record conversations. There is no reason for an interviewer to question or challenge the views of participants. The point of an interview is to gain each participant's perspective. One major problem with interviews is interviewer bias, which includes not just active bias but also passive bias, such as an inability to consider all the possible questions that could be asked. This is why critical friends are helpful when constructing an interview agenda.

Focus groups

In its simplest sense, a focus group is a collection of people brought together in one place to discuss a specific topic. The researcher uses a small list of questions, focused on the topic, to generate discussion, and records the group's discussion as her data. The data from focus groups are much like data from interviews. The difference, obviously, is that a group of people contributes to the data, and this can produce a broader range of data than individual interviews. For Morgan (1988), the group interaction inherent in focus groups produces "data and insights that would be less accessible without the interaction found in a group" (p. 12).

The strengths and limitations of focus groups as a method of data collection depend on you and your research task. What works well in one situation might be inappropriate in another.

A first consideration is that focus groups require a degree of skill to facilitate. As Punch (2009) affirms, "The role of the researcher changes in a group interview, functioning more as a moderator or facilitator, and less as an interviewer" (p. 147). If you are going to conduct a focus group yourself, you should be a person who is confident in your people skills—especially your group-work skills. A good facilitator is sensitive to the group's mood and knows how to draw out participants (some are more reticent than others). Where tensions arise in the group (and this can happen), a strong facilitator can mediate or diffuse them once they are out in the open, or even turn such tensions into productive insights. The facilitator should also be able to keep the group on track. Sticking to the focus group's agenda while allowing sufficient space to explore ideas thoroughly can be a real art.

If this list of responsibilities seems overwhelming, consider having someone else facilitate your focus group while you take on a different role. You can cofacilitate the group or perhaps act as an observer. Being freed from the facilitation role by handing it over to a trusted colleague allows you to gain a wealth of information with the time and energy you can then devote to direct observation.

Another consideration is that focus groups tend to provide in-depth information. In other words, use them to explore one or two topics thoroughly, not to answer a long list of questions. One mistake we've seen in focus groups is an overambitious agenda. The researcher becomes dismayed when the focus group hunkers down on one or two key issues; at the session's end, he finds he has terrific information, but only on two of the six questions he'd hoped to cover.

In addition, focus groups generate a unique *quality* of data. A good focus-group conversation creates synergy, and can reveal insights and generate creative responses you might not otherwise have the opportunity to learn about. Focus-group work has a spontaneity that makes its outcomes highly credible. On the dark side, however, poor group dynamics can create unpleasant and unproductive experiences. Sometimes creativity and spontaneity prompt negative or downright unethical conduct by participants.

It's good to remember that focus groups deliver a great deal of data from a number of people. They are generally inexpensive and fairly easy to organize. However, a number of researchers have found their attempts to organize focus groups hampered by the busy schedules of diverse participants from different locations. You might consider sticking to a setting that minimizes logistical difficulties—say, all participants are from one organization and the group is held during a workday.

Surveys

Surveys allow researchers to acquire data and opinions from a population. This could be an entire population (like the population of Canada in the federal government's census) or a representative sample of a population. Surveys can be a useful tool for both public- and private-sector organizations and leaders: government, health care providers, universities, private businesses, and others. Because of their versatility, surveys are a meat-and-potatoes-type staple of many research tasks.

Surveys can be broad in scope and content, reaching large groups and gathering large quantities of statistical data with relative speed and ease. For example, researchers may want to discover some part of the public's opinion about school programs, political issues, consumer products, or a variety of other topics. The process is simple, actually: figure out what you want to know and whom you want to ask, then write a series of questions that would elicit the information you need. Once this information is obtained, it can be used to make decisions, develop new programs, improve service, influence decision makers, and so on. The number of people who want to gain insight about topics is almost endless.

Surveys are used for one simple reason: researchers cannot interview everyone. As a result, they try to find a "representative sample" of the group they want to gain information from or about, and then assume that this sample represents the thousands (or sometimes even millions) of people who have similar opinions and preferences. Researchers assume that the opinion of a respondent is similar to the opinion of those people the respondent speaks for. For example, if you want to gain a general sense of what a group of people think, you might ask a large number of them using a survey instrument. These data can be used to gain insight into trends or relationships, to generally understand attitudes or behaviours, or to make decisions about the next step in a research agenda.

A survey instrument might ask if participants would like to be involved in individual interviews that focus more specifically on the topic in question. In this way, a researcher could identify a smaller group of potential interviewees. Individual interviews can be used to flesh out the information gained in the broader survey questions.

As with any data-collection method, researchers must conduct their surveys in an ethical manner. That means that they must respect the participants' right to privacy or nonparticipation. As a survey researcher, you should never divulge the identity of your participants, their personal information, or their specific answers unless you have their permission in writing to do so. A clear and informative cover letter should accompany any survey you use, and it should explain rights and ethical considerations to participants.

Surveys may be simple—for example, we have seen a wonderful five-question survey—but can be complex in their application. They are almost always question-forced answer in format, and the data can be collected by phone, mail, in person, and—increasingly today—over the Internet. The goal of surveys is always to collect data from a large number of people.

Sometimes, surveys used in site-based research can be passive. For example, one teacher set up a survey on a website used by the sort of participants he wanted to be part of his study. The survey was brief but continued throughout an entire year. This survey was not his only data-collecting tool, but it added a further *triangulated* insight into his work.

Observation
Observation allows the researcher to examine the setting and natural environment of participants. Remember that context is important. Examining the context involves looking carefully and writing clear,

detailed descriptions. Observation is always valuable, but has some drawbacks, such as interrupting or disturbing participants.

If you choose this data-collection method, you need to decide the degree to which you, the observer, will be interacting with your research subjects. Your involvement will depend on the goals of your observation, the expectations and wishes of your research subjects, and your own familiarity with the research environment. Some examples here may help.

Observing without interaction

A researcher is studying principals' leadership qualities. He observes a staff meeting, but sits quietly in the corner, taking notes, because he wants to see how the principal and teachers relate and make decisions during the meeting. Here, his involvement might interfere with this goal.

Observing with interaction

A researcher is evaluating the effectiveness of the services offered at an outreach school in a rural community. Statistics reveal which programs are used the most or the least, but don't tell her much about how students view the programs or why they access them. To learn more, the researcher spends several afternoons as a volunteer in the school, observing how students work, and visiting with them. The process enriches her understanding of the school and helps her to build trusting relationships with its students in preparation for interviews she hopes to conduct later in her study.

Again, it is less a question of whether your direct involvement (or what is usually called *participant observation*) will influence the actions of your research subjects. Simply put, it will. Rather, ask whether your interaction with the people you are observing will further your research objective or hinder it. As you can see from the examples above, each case will present unique needs and responses.

The important thing for researchers to remember is that, interacting or not, observations are always shaped to some degree by your own biases. Simple awareness of this fact will help you to represent what you see and hear more fairly. Another possibility is to have another person involved in your project undertake the observations with you, creating a second perspective and set of notes. Follow up by comparing your findings with the other person.

Document analysis

Document analysis originated from the idea of hermeneutical learning. Hermeneutics is the study of written text, a practice that began with the Bible because people wanted to understand what the Bible had to teach modern people. The hermeneutic researcher asks three questions:

- What does/do the story/text/words mean? (Define the terms.)
- What did the story/text/words mean to the audience who originally heard it? (In biblical terms, for those who first listened to the parables, for example.)
- What do these stories/texts/words mean for us today?

These same questions can be asked of photos, symbols, or cultural artifacts. Take, for example, a Calvin Klein magazine ad. Who is in the ad? Man or woman? Thin or not? Long hair or short? Young or old? What is the ad for? Perfume sample—if so, why? What does this say about the need to smell good? How is the person clothed, and so what? What does all of this—synthesized—tell us about our culture and society? And this said, what should we do with it?

What else might be a "document" for document analysis? For example, hockey referees wear black-and-white-striped uniforms. Perhaps this is a not-so-obvious *reference* (note the same root word as *referee*) to the yin-yang sorts of calls that a hockey ref must make in a game. Is one call by a referee good (symbolized in our society by white) and another bad (symbolized by black)? Was our society racially thoughtless in its use of black and white to symbolize good and bad? Another example: a university symbolizes itself using an icon of a castle, which is an interesting juxtaposition given the university's attempt to gain a reputation for innovative, online programming. Might this icon impact the culture of the institution? That would be a document-analysis question—and you could investigate it further through the photos of learners in the university's handbook and advertising.

You can see the possibilities for studies of schools. How can your school logo or motto be interpreted? Does it really represent the values of the school? The point of document analysis is to find significant information embedded in what the organization you are studying has created. Even the advertisements a school chooses or the way it arranges and uses its physical space—including how the principal shapes her office and what sorts of pictures are on the walls—are "documents" that can tell much about what that organization really values.

It is probably fair to say that all action research tasks could include the study and analysis of documents. Document analysis can be used as a single method of research or to help you triangulate data in a supplemental way.

Document analysis differs from other research methods in two major ways. First, it is *indirect* research: it studies human beings by studying something they have made or written, not by studying the human beings themselves. Second, it is *unobtrusive*. Because documents are not human, they do not react as humans might. Philosophically, document analysis assumes documents are created from the perspectives of those who create them. These perspectives can be explicit, but are often implicit. We also assume that, by studying documents carefully and fully, we might come to understand deeper meanings within these documents—whether the documents are created by official sources, such as policy statements written by school leaders, or from personal accounts, such as letters to parents or even the minutes of meetings. Finally, we also assume that documents exist for some purpose, and knowing these purposes can help us understand and interpret the research situation in a richer way.

Document analysis has some advantages: it is generally inexpensive; the data never alter and can be reanalyzed; understandings can be compared over time, culture, and context; computer programs can be used to help analyze text when researchers establish rules for coding texts.

Document analysis has some disadvantages, too. In particular, it can be time-consuming.

A document epiphany

Jim's initial love for document analysis arose many years ago during a flight from Phoenix to Dallas. The flight was short and passengers were given a small basket that included a sandwich and a soft drink and some chips. But what was so great about the basket was the little paper doily that separated the food from the basket. The doily was a throwaway, but it was beautifully designed. The design was cut paper, perfectly systematic and organized. In fact, the designer had copyrighted the design—his name was on the back with the copyright date. Jim wrote:

> Suddenly, I was amazed by what I was seeing. Our culture had honoured creativity by allowing a creator to register the creation. The man had probably sent his mother a copy (if she was alive). The aesthetic of the paper was a system of round and, to my mind, beautiful squiggles and paper pressings, perfectly formed and repeated across the face of the small paper. And this artistic creation was being used in a specific function—and it was temporary. The flight attendant was actually moving up and down the aisle, tossing these beautiful and heartfelt (the man was obviously proud, hence the copyright) creation away.
>
> No one seemed as panicked as I was about this travesty. So I gently put the paper doily into my briefcase, where it stayed for years and was a regular example of my research insight. From this "document," I moved on to analyzing magazine commercials

and layouts as cultural artifacts to lift out their cultural signifi-
cance. These days, whenever I teach research document analy-
sis, I ask students to analyze the cultural meanings of Canada
embedded in hockey cards.

Planning for good data

The central focus of your research plan or method is to lead you
through the collection of data and to do it effectively, efficiently,
and ethically. Successful data collection in all research projects is
developed around three simple questions:

- What data are to be collected?
- How will the data be collected?
- Who or what sources will provide the data?

The amount of data, or evidence, you gather will depend on how
big your research task is. Is your focus confined to a small group of
participants? Is your focus an entire organization, like a whole school
or business?

When doing any research, although there will be surprises, it is
best to determine which data are suitable before deciding how and
when to collect them. Therefore, a key step in developing your
research plan is to examine your alternatives. The choice is one part
pragmatic and one part ethical. What should you do? What are the
reasonable limits of what you can do?

A good first step is to figure out who knows what. If you can answer
this question, it is easier to list potential sources of data and from
whom data could be collected. Then, ask yourself which sources
answer your central research question and your subquestions most
directly. Next, prioritize these sources in terms of relevance and
importance to your study. Finally, ask yourself if there is anything
wrong (unethical) about asking these people to participate. For
example, will their participation harm them in some way?

The question of potential harm might be more of a problem than
it first seems. Here's an example, the like of which has happened
in more than one research project. A researcher sees a problem within
her organization. She develops a research plan, collects her data, and
drafts some preliminary findings. Her boss—in a higher management
position within this organization—reads the work. Frankly, it doesn't
sit well with him. This young upstart is talking about his company and
life, and is spelling out the difficulties that her research will solve.
The boss is angry and feels blamed. He reads on to see complaint
after complaint from employees who participated in the research—
all people the boss thought were loyal workers in the company.

Can you see where this is going? The reader's bias (in this case, a good thing because he loves the organization) is so strong that the work can never be read without personal engagement. As a researcher, never forget you are dealing with people's lives. These people, especially if they are good at their work, are invested in what you are studying. Therefore, they are interested in your research. That's what makes the research worth doing. It is also what makes doing the research a delicate proposition. So, do research delicately and with consideration for yourself, your organization, and your participants.

Once you have chosen and prioritized your sources of data, you will have a better idea of what data you might gather easily and what data might be more difficult to collect. Eventually your research plan should include a description of the data you will use, and how and when you will gather it.

A final consideration, and one many researchers forget, is how to report your data. Remember that reporting research is part of doing research, not something that comes after the research is done. Choose data-collection methods that will deliver data that already look like something you can report systematically.

Writing your research plan

With any good research, it is important that researchers obtain data from a wide variety of sources. Such *triangulation* strengthens the validity of the information obtained. In site-based action research, data are gathered for different purposes at different points in the process. Baseline data determine the extent of a problem ("How big is the problem?") and clarify the existing situation ("What is going on?"). Research data measure the impact of the intervention ("Am I making a difference? Is the situation changing?").

The above questions are crucial, and you need to ask and answer each one when you begin to structure and write your own research plan. As a teacher, this part is easy because you are used to writing lesson plans. Writing your research plan is like writing a detailed lesson plan. For those who are not teachers, think about the directions for putting IKEA furniture together. They are specific, and your research plan should be specific—like fitting nuts with bolts.

There are always choices about how much specificity to include, and you could choose to write your research plan with less specificity. However, you would be wrong to do so. Research should be fun, but, because you are working with participants who must be protected, you are ethically bound to conduct research well. To be slapdash would be simply unethical.

So, how should you begin to write your research plan? The answer is to think about all the things—each and every activity—you must do if you are to do your data collection well, and write them down as a series of specific steps. Then review these steps to see if anything is missing. Next, give the steps (your method) to a critical friend and ask him to read them. Can he follow the process? Is a step confusing? If so, look at it again. It is tough to think of everything, especially the first time you work out data-collection methods. You have heard this from us before: a critical friend is helpful.

The National Staff Development Council (2000, p. 2) suggests that a researcher should work to specify her data-collection process by following this procedure:

- Match data sources to the central research question.
- Collect data from as many sources as possible.
- Keep a data log that includes the date, time, and information collected.
- Organize your data around themes, key issues, or topics.

A sample research plan

The following is an example of a research plan for a project about teacher mentoring. Notice the detail and the steps. Although things change and surprises happen once you begin to collect your data (all research is filled with change and the need to make quick, by-the-seat-of-your-pants decisions—that's life), the point is to try to think of everything before setting out on the work.

1. Generate a profile of the chosen school division, including:
   - key administrative personnel—division website, phone calls, personal visit/meetings
   - student population: breakdowns by school and grade, class size—division website, publications
   - teaching staff: breakdowns by grade, subject, and seniority—division website, publications
   - geography of division (school locations and settings)—maps, division website and publications
   - incomes and demography of residents in division—statistics from division (division publications, website) from census (library, online), from municipality (municipal publications, online)
2. Consider issues that may emerge from this profile. Are there reasons not to use this division for the research? Do any practical issues present themselves?
3. Identify key people in the division who I can consult about teacher mentorship, and who can help focus my research questions and provide useful guidance.

4. Determine the perceptions of the division regarding current and future teacher mentorship challenges. Using the division profile and the guidance of key people in the division, consider:
    –   interviews—this could form most of the research, or part of it in combination with a survey or focus groups. This would be a good technique to use if a few people already have experience mentoring, or have formed clear ideas about it.
    –   a survey—this might be useful if it seems like broad patterns are important. Teachers might have different perceptions than division administrators, or senior teachers might have different perceptions than newer teachers. Consider how to structure survey questions to capture such differences.
    –   focus groups—this might be useful to crystallize key perceptions held by different groups of teachers or administrators. Consider how many focus groups might be useful, how to pull the right people together.
5. Consider what data-collection methods would be best in terms of quality of data. Consider what methods would be best in practical terms (time, effort, cost).
6. Collect and analyze the data. Consider foreseeable issues/problems and areas requiring priority attention as perceived by the division.
7. Revisit the literature review. Draft some preliminary findings in an initial report.
8. Share preliminary findings with a small group of school district leaders. Get feedback. Revise report.
9. Share revised report with key district committees: the advisory committee on mentorship that will be established by the district, the curriculum committee, the leader/trainee selection committee, and the committee responsible for funding. Get feedback and continue to revise report.
10. Submit a complete draft of report to district leadership. Get feedback and finalize report.

Tips for keeping your plan workable

Keep your focus. Start focused, and stay focused, on your central question and subquestions as you write your plan. Do your literature review. Read others' completed research to find out what data exist, and to refine your questions and method. Depend on your research "ancestors" and build on their work.

Cast a wide net. Plan to use multiple data sources or data-collection methods. Triangulation helps you locate your central, guiding target.

Make a flexible plan. You should make a detailed plan, but the details shouldn't box you in.

- Planning is a process. Trust the process.
- Make your plan flexible enough to guide your evolving inquiry without stunting its growth. The plan is a map, not the territory.
- Though a plan is a representation of what will happen if events remain under your control, you can never fully control events, nor would you want to.
- Having a plan will help you adjust should any ethical and other hazards arise on the trail.

Keep moving forward. Avoid overanalyzing or getting stuck in one spot of the plan. Your plan will evolve as you get better at research; it will change as your inquiry progresses. Expect these changes, and don't panic. Consider the steps of your research plan carefully, but don't make it so detailed that you don't begin your research. Find the balance: do your plan thoroughly and thoughtfully, but focus your energies on the research, not the planning. Some people are particular in their planning, and never begin the actual work. Begin!

Start thinking through next steps. When hiking—especially up a mountain—it is always satisfying to stop, catch your breath, and take a look at how far you've come. Sometimes you pull out the trail map to gain some perspective on where you are.

Finishing a research plan is a good place to pause, enjoy, and look around. You've got a good piece of trail behind you now, and that should feel good. You can also see the trail in front of you more clearly: How far can you see down it? At this point, you can begin to engage some practical questions that will affect how you will manage your work and hone its impact.

- What key decisions do you need to make?
- Who can help you?
- What resources do you need?
- What are realistic timelines?
- What outcomes do you really want to see?
- What are the best measures for those outcomes?

We look at these questions in detail in Chapter 7.

Ask for help. If you run into problems, ask someone you respect for advice. You are part of a community of scholars. You have made critical friends—use them. Find a strong mentor. If you can find someone to help, this person may be able to offer critical feedback to you during your research implementation. Having a plan also helps you explain to them what your difficulty is and just where you are on the trail.

Make sure your central question is important. Writing a research plan is important work, and you need to take time to do it well. But drafting a research plan is still an early stage in the process of completing a research project. It's a good time to re-evaluate your central research question and subquestions.

The quality of a study depends mostly on the quality of the research questions that frame it. Your own satisfaction with the questions you've chosen is the best reason to invest the time, energy, and resources of others. Pursuing a topic because you feel you "should" is always tempting; however, if the topic doesn't truly engage you, you will lack the time, energy, and focus needed to complete your work.

It's worth taking the time

You probably could have figured out everything we wrote in this chapter for yourself. Perhaps it seems too easy, or maybe you feel that research must be more complex. But remember that the everyday ways researchers use to collect data are really just this simple. The research road is not tough—but walking it *well* can be difficult. When researchers mess up, it is generally because they are sloppy or inconsiderate, not because of the data-collection methods themselves. So walk slowly, be thoughtful as you take in the sights, and devote the time and patience necessary to thoroughly document your research journey.

6

From plan to action

ESSENTIAL QUESTIONS

How do you turn plans into actions? What's the next step?

CHAPTER PURPOSE

To clarify what parts of the research process this book has covered so far, through the metaphor of vacation planning

This chapter is just a little breather—a short vacation!

Take a moment to envision what happens when you plan a vacation. First, you recognize a desire (or, in some cases, need) for a getaway, and begin to narrow the when and where. Maybe you're travelling with your family, and you find that summer is the best time to go, considering school vacation dates. Then, you take into account a multitude of variables—time, cost, age of your children, past vacation experiences—and decide that you're going to make the trip of a lifetime.

Now the real planning begins. You begin to research different trip routes, including stops. You consult relatives, post questions to your Facebook and Twitter friends, research possible destinations en route, visit a travel agency, refer to travel guides and brochures, all to learn about your vacation destination. You start to develop a general plan for what your family wants, considering their wishes and the time available.

Following this, the planning gets more specific. You could stay at a resort to visit your destination, but you decide this is unrealistic for your budget. However, if you plan carefully, you can stay elsewhere and save several hundred dollars. You map exactly which highways to travel and identify motels where you will spend your nights. You book accommodations, determine realistic budgets, and find places your family can visit along the way. Soon, the day of departure is here and all your preparation is about to pay off.

Research and vacations have things in common

This vacation metaphor helps illustrate the first steps in preparing for action research—steps we have so far covered in this book.

First, action research can, and should, be initiated by teachers in site-based contexts, as they identify questions to investigate related to teaching and learning. Just as a vacation can be planned without the assistance of a travel agent, a research project can be designed and accomplished without having a PhD or access to a huge research grant. Preparing for action research begins with a desire to investigate a question, accompanied by the belief that the question you investigate can be answered with academic rigour and, when answered, will add knowledge to the greater educational community. These beliefs serve as the foundation for any teacher-led action research project. You must recognize that the first step in any process is recognizing a need and determining an action. Just as the declaration "We should take a vacation!" serves as a catalyst for planning a holiday, the statement "I wonder…" is the starting point for action research.

Determining the destination

With vacation planning, the desire to travel is just the beginning. The next step is determining the destination. Occasionally, this process is simple and clear. Often, however, the decision requires investigation. Prospective travellers determine their general desire, then they narrow their choice by searching the Internet, talking with friends and coworkers, or skimming travel brochures.

This process parallels what you do in your research task.

Occasionally, the research question emerges clearly at the outset. In Chapter 1, we shared four profiles of site-based researchers. In one profile, Martin, the head of a mathematics department, wanted to investigate "flipped classrooms." His research question was well defined early in the exploratory process: "Could the flipped-classroom concept become a model for effective mathematics instruction in our department?" He went on to refine this question through a series of subquestions, but the overarching focus for the research was clear from the start.

However, researchers often develop their research questions through further investigation. In another profile, Pamela was interested in the reading habits of the primary students in her classroom and the development of early reading skills. She did not have a clear initial research question. It emerged as Pamela investigated the research literature.

Investigating possibilities

In vacation planning, deeper exploration comes by examining information and engaging in conversations related to your destination. As part of this phase, you may read travel brochures and books, explore the Internet, and talk with family and acquaintances. As you learn more, you may alter your plans and investigate new possibilities for your trip.

Like this phase in vacation planning, literature reviews have symbiotic relationships with your research questions: your questions guide the sources of information you engage, and the sources of information help shape the nature of your research.

In vacation planning, reviewing travel magazines can help refine hotel destinations. In action research, literature reviews can reveal processes and insights congruent with questions you want to answer. And the literature is constantly growing, as site-based researchers add to the knowledge about your area of interest.

Refining your plans

You have made the decision to take a trip. You've figured out your destination. You've read up on where you might stay and what you might do when you get to your destination.

Now, you need to make decisions on what you *will* do and where you *will* stay. You need to get specific. How much time and money do you have? What activities best match the collective interests of your family? These factors come into play as you move forward, until a well-defined vacation plan takes shape.

Such planning resembles designing the research method for your research task. You know the questions you want to ask. Now you need to know how you will answer them. Again, you need to get specific. What data should you collect? How will you collect it? What will keep the work manageable? As you work through these issues, you develop your research plan—the core of what you will do to find out what you want to know.

What's next?

As exciting as planning a trip might be, planning is obviously not the ultimate goal. You want to take the actual trip.

Taking the trip means putting those plans into action—getting to your destination and doing what you planned to do—and this involves a broader set of practicalities. For example, you may need some luggage. Your kids may need some games for the car. You may need to stop the paper delivery, and arrange for someone to pick up the mail.

In terms of your research task, this is more or less the point we have reached—the point where plans turn into action and practicalities become your focus. This is your next step and the next chapter in this book.

The chapters you have already read aimed to prepare you for site-based action research. The next chapters are about conducting that research.

Enjoy the trip! And stay flexible. What if it rains the day you planned to visit the beach? Know that you can change your plan as you move forward, and work out a different way to reach your objectives.

7

Managing your research project

ESSENTIAL QUESTIONS

What is project management?

How can the ideas of project management further action research?

CHAPTER PURPOSE

To highlight key elements of project management

To describe the purpose and process of creating a project schedule

In Chapter 1 through Chapter 5, we mostly discussed your research task in terms of a question that needs an answer. To be successful with your task, you also need to think about it as a *project* that needs *management.*

Project management is a discipline with its own paradigms and gurus. In this chapter, we are going to cherry-pick some of its common-sense, key ideas. As researchers, we have found these ideas useful in converting our plans into actions.

In his classic *Pedagogy of Hope,* Paulo Freire (1995) defined literacy as diminishing the distance between dreaming and doing. The world is filled with great ideas gone wrong because those with the idea didn't move well from the *dream of the idea* to the *do of the idea.* Research tasks are no different. And with research tasks involving children, it is crucially important to move consciously, deliberately, and well from *dream* to *do.*

Key elements of project management

Project management helps you *identify* what you need to do, and then *schedule* what you need to do.

"What you need to do" includes practical matters that you may not yet have considered as part of your research task. But the list begins at a familiar place: with setting objectives.

Setting project objectives

In many ways, you have already done substantial thinking about the objectives of your task by defining your central research question and subquestions, and by designing your research method. But your task probably also has a larger objective, to do with resolving an issue arising from your classroom or your organization—as an action researcher, this kind of site-based, specific problem is what triggered the research in the first place. Ultimately, your objective is to bring about change for the better.

You could say that your task is a *research project*, where the *research* is about answering a question, and the *project* is about effecting change. Setting *project objectives* helps you strategize how you will effect change.

In project management, objectives are crucial because they help those who work on the project: (1) define the final outcome; (2) create a point of reference for their contributions; (3) create a basis for evaluation that helps pull together their insights.

Most teachers are familiar with the "SMART" method of setting objectives. In project management, SMART objectives are "key performance indicators"—ways to make sure what you're doing will lead to the useful result you want.

SMART stands for **s**pecific, **m**easurable, **a**ttainable, **r**elevant, and **t**ime sensitive.

SPECIFIC: WHAT *EXACTLY* DO YOU WISH TO ACCOMPLISH?

Canfield and Switzer's (2005) *The Success Principles* states, "Vague goals produce vague results" (p. 67). There is no place in research projects for vagueness. Canfield and Switzer believe vagueness eventually allows subconscious thoughts to become the focus—if project objectives are ambiguous or incomplete, their results will also be ambiguous or incomplete.

Another reason for detailed, clear project objectives is because others need to understand *what* you intend to accomplish with your research and *how* you will accomplish it.

MEASURABLE: HOW WILL YOU *ASSESS* YOUR PROJECT'S SUCCESS?

It is always wise to set objectives you can measure. If you can't measure your progress, you can't track where you've been and adjust your next steps. Measurable objectives have this characteristic: you can break them down into indicators that show change in the direction of your desired outcome.

What is a true indicator of progress toward your objective? Select a standard indicator—one you will apply consistently over the course of your project. In educational research projects, you might choose student engagement as an indicator (however you choose to measure engagement) or student learning (again, however you choose to measure learning).

ATTAINABLE: IS YOUR RESEARCH PROJECT *MANAGEABLE*?

Having personal goals that stretch you is important, but projects should always be manageable. In other words, your project objectives should be realistic for your needs and context. Many new researchers, with every good intention, set unrealistically lavish objectives—and their projects never get done. What seasoned researchers know that new researchers do not know is how rich data can be. Creating unattainable goals is disempowering and only serves to demotivate your work. Remember to set high but realistic goals. In the same vein, objectives that are too easily accomplished do not stretch your capacities or allow your project to have as much impact as it could. We encourage you to find that right mix of challenge and possibility. The best way we have found to assess this point is to share your work with a trusted colleague.

RELEVANT: DOES YOUR RESEARCH PROJECT TARGET A PROBLEM OR ISSUE YOU *REALLY WANT* TO RESOLVE?

Reaching objectives is great, except when the objectives are trivial. What is the underlying purpose of your research? How can you create objectives that are in line with your organization's mission statement or purpose? Relevant objectives ensure you are dedicating your effort on what your organization counts as crucial. Objectives should be relevant.

We would argue that, when engaging in site-based action research, the relevance question is best addressed by asking, "What impact will this project have on students?" If the answer suggests minimal impact, it is unlikely you have chosen a relevant objective. The research you are planning to undertake needs to ensure that student learning and/or engagement are at the core.

TIME SENSITIVE: WHAT *DEADLINES* ARE REASONABLE FOR COMPLETING YOUR RESEARCH PROJECT?

Any project objective you shape must allow for time. Unless you are extremely self-motivated, ignoring the element of time can encourage procrastination. The advantage research projects have over other projects is that they include a research method or plan—step-by-step procedures for collecting data. Your method, if you have done your work well, already contains thinking about timing and deadlines. We encourage all researchers to be wise when outlining their method and their path to project completion, and to follow those outlines well—unless something better or worse happens.

Building a budget

The budget for your project is an itemized list of the resources you need to complete your project, with estimates of what each item will cost.

In project management, the three major resource and cost categories are labour, materials, and other direct or indirect costs.

Labour, as a cost, is about who you need to hire. You need to ask yourself whether you can do all the work your project entails on your own, or whether you should ask assistants to run some parts of the project for you.

When teachers are asked to list their scarcest resource, they generally say time. Sometimes, new teacher-researchers will say knowledge. It is not that creating and running a research project is difficult per se—it is just that doing anything the first few times is difficult. These costs must be attended to as part of any teacher-led research project. You may have time and skill deficits that you need to fill.

For example, your site-based research may involve surveying a large population of students. Do you have time to see this through properly, or should you hire someone to deliver the survey and collate the results?

Or, your research may involve engaging a technology unfamiliar to you, such as a new form of social media. Would it make sense to hire an expert to help you?

Materials are the tools and equipment you need to do your research project, from start to finish. For example, you may need:

- handouts (paper, photocopying)
- recording devices
- a computer lab with 20 stations
- venues for meetings

Be as precise and thorough as you can. Note what tools and equipment you will need to buy or rent.

Other costs include direct and indirect costs you may incur by doing the project. For example, do you need to travel for the project? This could involve transportation and accommodation costs. Do you need time away from the classroom to conduct your research? If so, you will need a substitute teacher.

As you complete your itemized list, consider how you will meet the needs and costs you have identified. Could your organization provide support? Do you need to look for outside funds or resources?

Developing a team

Even if you decide to do all or most of the work your research project entails on your own, you still need a team of people. Research, as we have said before, is about relationships, including relationships between people and people, and between people and knowledge. Relationships are especially important in action research, because the objectives and method of the research are often negotiated between the researcher and the researched.

So, it's vital to think about who you need to communicate with:

- Who are your major stakeholders?
- Who should be "in the know" about your research project and provide insight as your research project proceeds?

You may also decide that you need help with your project, for reasons of time, resources, or expertise:

- Who has skills that you need? (This could include people you hire, as well as people you consult.)
- Who has resources you need?

Finally, all projects need evaluation as they progress and at their conclusion:

- Who should evaluate the project?

Each member of your team should have a formal role in the work, in some way—for example, as a member of a steering committee, as a hands-on assistant, as a reviewer. There are many ways to structure and coordinate a team. You need to be clear on what your structure will be, and on the role each team member has within the structure.

CHARACTERISTICS OF TEAM MEMBERS

The members of your research project team are the keys to making a research project run smoothly. When putting together your team, we encourage you to look for members with the following characteristics:

- They possess the technical competence needed to do the work.
- They are politically sensitive.
- They are problem-focused and goal-oriented.
- They have high self-esteem.
- They like people and can foster and maintain good community.

- They have the ability to communicate directly with team members.
- They avoid interpersonal dramas.

The project manager is the centre of the project team, its most important member. For site-based action research, the project manager is likely to be you.

The Project Management Institute Educational Foundation (2012) suggests that project managers have four main responsibilities: leading the planning of a project; getting needed resources in place; working with the project team to overcome known and unforeseen obstacles; and leading the project as it proceeds. Some of these responsibilities involve acting as a supervisor; some involve acting as a facilitator. Experienced project managers make conscious choices about how to act depending on what needs doing.

Project managers need to be good at negotiating, resolving conflicts, encouraging others to work as a team, and fostering communication. (In this, they are like teachers—so you already have lots of these skills at hand.) Successful project managers strive to demonstrate technical and administrative credibility; political and interpersonal sensitivity; and ethical and systematic decision making.

There are two project pitfalls that project managers should know in advance and try to avoid. Although Michael Fullan (2010) supports the creativity of a "ready, fire, aim" approach to project management, projects suffer when leaders consistently act before thinking. On the other hand, projects also can suffer from "paralysis by analysis" when project managers think so much that no one ever acts.

PLANNING FOR SYSTEMATIC REVIEW

We encourage you to embrace review and evaluation of your research project as a regular aspect of your work. Review can take the form of regular feedback from your project team. It should also involve more formal evaluations by people you specifically recruit as reviewers.

It is wise to build review and evaluation into your research project from the outset:

Set up regular "check in" points, where you provide updates on the project to your team, and obtain feedback.

Establish how you will communicate with your team—for example, in face-to-face meetings, by e-mails, or some combination.

Track the activities and progress of the project in a clear and structured way, so you can provide useful updates. You could do this by keeping a weekly journal, for example.

Establish when more formal reviews will take place and what reviewers will evaluate. For example, will they evaluate "chapters" of a final report as you write them? Will you produce updates of the project specifically for reviewers?

Set up procedures for final evaluation of the project, including:

- collecting "lessons learned" from members of the project team
- collecting perspectives on project outcomes from research participants
- engaging in self-review of your own work
- getting a formal review of your final report

ABOUT REVIEWERS

Reviewers have a role in your research project separate from your project team. Their job is to provide a fresh, critical, and knowledgeable perspective—an informed outsiders' reaction to the purpose, direction, and quality of your work. We suggest that you find people—it could be just one person—who has:

- experience with research supervision (how a research team should work)
- experience with your research methodology (how your research should work)
- experience with project management (how standards of work should be governed, how resources should be used, how problem solving should proceed)

Envisioning the final products

Sometime soon, if you have not done this already, you need to ask: "What will my project deliver as its final products?" This raises the question: "What *could* my project deliver?" Although the products of a research project always include a written report, the report might not be the most important part. This is especially true for action research projects, because they arise from specific problems and issues whose resolution could take any number of possible forms. The right choice for your project depends on your needs and the needs of your organization.

For example, action research projects could deliver unit plans, workshops, evaluation protocols, newly designed curriculum packages, or lists of best practices. Your project objective—your need to effect change—shapes what your project delivers, which is exactly how it should be.

That said, you do also need to produce a report, because other people will want to know about your project.

Our guess is that you will underestimate how important your research might be to others. The idea that others should use your work as a model for their own might seem farfetched. But that often happens. We encourage you to not be surprised that other teachers will be interested in your work. First, some may be interested in the content (what you found). Second, some may be interested in your method (what you did). When you read the research literature, you were interested in what others did. Now you are becoming part of that same research literature—you are working as a scholar. For us, this is the most compelling reason to do your work well.

Creating a project schedule

Figuring out what to do and when to do it is key to project management. In any project, some activities might be done at the same time; others must be done in a sequence. It is wise to know which activities are which, and creating a schedule is part of sorting this out.

From this chapter and previous chapters, you know your research project has these elements: data collection, resources, a team, systematic review, reviewers, a written report, and potentially other final products on point for you and your organization.

With this in mind, draft a schedule. You can do this on a spreadsheet or by using a paper "storyboard" approach. We have described the storyboard approach, below.

- Write down the research project's major objective. Write down how the research project attends to this objective. (Two sentences.)
- Divide the research project into its major steps. Write each step on a separate piece of paper, and write what needs to be done to complete each step. (Two sentences for each step.) Mark each step with a different colour (you could use highlighters or sticky dots).
- Sequence the major steps (by shuffling the papers). This will be a rough sequence.
- Break down each major step into substeps. Write down what you need to do to complete each substep. (Use outline form, and use separate pieces of paper for each substep. Consider what resources and people you need to muster and assign as part of creating substeps.) Mark each substep with the colour of its organizing major step.
- Add a "time budget" to each substep (estimate how long each substep will take).

- Sequence the substeps within each major step, answering the question: "What has to be done before the next substep can happen?"
- Review the sequence. Consider the following questions, and reshuffle as necessary:
  - With all the substeps spelled out, do some of them fit more logically in a different part of the sequence?
  - Could some parts of the sequence be done concurrently?

- Review the sequence again to consider (if you have not done this already) where to schedule review points with your team and evaluation points with formal reviewers. Add these into the sequence. (Note that this might generate new substeps about preparing for review and evaluation points.)
- Put the sequence on a timeline with dates, paying attention to the time you budgeted for each substep. Write this timeline out. Use the colours to identify when you are working on parts of each major step, as necessary.
- Share your draft schedule with a supportive colleague. Listen to the insights this colleague brings to your work.

Features of an effective schedule

Your schedule is your foundation for action: for conducting your research and completing your project. To be effective, your schedule needs to say "yes" to the following questions:
- Are the major research project activities identified and listed in succession and in detail?
- Are the types and quantities of resources identified for each activity?
- Are the activities defined in terms of their predecessors (what should happen before the activity begins) and durations (how long they should take)?
- Are research project milestones identified in appropriate detail?
- Are individuals or groups assigned tasks that, if undertaken well, would completely perform all the work needed to complete the research project?

Writing a project overview

To build your team, recruit reviewers, and raise resources, you need to be able to communicate to others what your project is about, both succinctly and in detail.

The succinct description is something you should be able to carry around in your head. Some people think of it as an "elevator speech" —something you could tell others between when an elevator shuts its doors and when it opens them at the next stop.

Most people write a project overview to give the detailed description. Overviews briefly describe the objectives of the project, its deliverables, and its milestones. It's really a way of reworking and re-presenting the plan you have made to manage your project well. Reworking and re-presenting is always a useful exercise, because it helps build your confidence and fluency with the process of doing your project.

You can build an overview with sections that answer the following questions:

Rationale: Why you are undertaking this project?

Objectives: What educational impacts do you expect the project to have?

Final products: What will your project produce as final products?

Schedule: What are the major milestones of the project? When do you expect to reach them?

Communications plan: Who will receive updates and have input as the project proceeds (e.g., stakeholders, team members)? How will this communication take place?

Budget: What resources and funds do you need to complete your project?

Keep your overview as brief as possible—aim for a thousand words—so that busy people can scan it quickly. Detail is your friend and your enemy: you need enough to show how interesting your project is and how competent you are, but too much detail is, well, too much.

Eight essential questions: a project-management checklist

We believe research projects that can answer these eight questions have a great chance of success.

Question 1: Does the project make sense to someone outside your research? For example, can another teacher in your district understand what your research project does and why this research project should be undertaken?

Question 2: Is there sufficient reason for others to be on board? Has broad ownership been sought? And, has the research project been discussed in ways that allow supporters to have input? (Note that we say *supporters*. We know there are always naysayers and, although their insights can be valuable, we encourage you not to let these people's bad attitudes disrupt your research plans.)

Question 3: Is it clear whose support or involvement is needed within the research project? Have those who need to be involved been invited to discuss the nature of their involvement?

Question 4: Does the research project have a specific plan of action? Do others know what this plan of action is? Have they had input? Do they agree?

Question 5: If you saw this research project with fresh eyes, would you be interested in planning, implementing, and managing the project?

Question 6: Have the nuts and bolts of the project (objectives, resources, research method, schedule) been reviewed and approved by everyone who should review and approve them?

Question 7: Are the specific steps that make up the research project outlined clearly? Would others know what should be done to complete the research project?

Question 8: Is the research project well defined? Is it clear what data the research project seeks and how it will evaluate that data? Does the research project have a definite beginning and ending date? Are all the costs (time, resources, money) clear? Is the research project manageable? Is it clear when the research project has been completed?

8

Collecting your data

ESSENTIAL QUESTIONS

What principles guide effective data collection?

What do the most common data-collection methods involve?

CHAPTER PURPOSE

To provide support to researchers in developing a variety of data-collection instruments and engaging in data-collection practices to support their research project

To share tips, advice, and templates related to effective data collection

Collecting data means doing the work needed to find out what you need to find out. Here is where the research rubber meets the road.

So far, in the "research part" of your research project, you have defined your area of interest; you have reviewed the related litera-ture; you have considered and decided on the questions you want to ask; and you have outlined who should be asked these questions, and how. Now, your plans become your actions. You are now at the stage of pulling all these ideas together into an action of discovery. You are ready to collect your data.

In Chapter 5, we shared the work of Todd Jick (1979), who identi-fied four simple fundamentals about data collection.

- Ask research participants directly.
- Ask research participants indirectly.

- Ask those who interact with the research participants.
- Observe the participants' actions or past actions.

These fundamentals frame your research plan, which lays out who you need to ask and how best to ask them. To review, your research should be focused on your specific needs; it should be organized in a systematic way; and it should ethically consider the needs of your participants. We believe research is a moral enterprise that should be done with consideration and care.

In this chapter, we identify and dissect a number of data-collection methods, providing our "IKEA versions," with consideration to the four fundamentals of data collection. We trust you will be able to understand these methods well enough to use them with confidence. We know the methods may change in their execution, and this is acceptable— in fact, it is common. Adjustments are often required to meet each research project's unique needs. There is almost always a difference between creating the vision and doing the work. The great Canadian literary critic Northrop Frye (1980) considered "desire versus reality" an entire literary genre. Within our caveat of focused, systematic, and ethical work, changes are acceptable and often necessary.

Principles of effective data collection

An important question to ask when venturing into data collection is, "Does the data already exist?" As Richard Sagor (2000) reminds us, "A good place to start looking for data is where data already exists. Only when existing data or artifacts are unavailable or inadequate is it necessary to create new instruments" (p. 76). Although the intent of this chapter is to provide guidance in designing instruments to collect data to support your research, give careful consideration to whether the questions you want to ask are already being asked or if the data you seek is already available. Perhaps your school division already administers a satisfaction survey for parents, asking valuable questions. Perhaps another school has already conducted interviews, with a format and set of questions that mirror the work you wish to accomplish. The old adage of "not reinventing the wheel" rings true when conducting site-based action research and should be a primary consideration before expending the time and energy involved in developing the methods and instruments we describe in this chapter.

A consideration to keep in mind when collecting your data is that "you cannot study everyone everywhere doing everything" (Miles & Huberman, 1994, p. 27). We often note that novice researchers attempt to access exceedingly large sample sizes, leading to increased difficulty when engaging in data collection and collating the data for analysis. To this end, we value developing manageable sample sizes and target groups. If you are researching the impact of parental involvement on student engagement, collect data from families from three schools rather than every school in the district. Interview a select group of students that represents a larger sample rather than attempting to schedule interview appointments for all students. Often, we have found in our research that "less is more." Statistically, the information you receive from a smaller sample or target group will reflect the information you would have received from a larger population. Careful attention to developing representative target groups can provide rich research data with less work.

We also recognize and encourage a "mixed methods" data-collection approach. You might administer a 10-question survey to high school students about what teaching strategies best engage them in their learning, followed by focused interviews of a sample of students to gain deeper insights into the same questions. You could then observe select classrooms to ascertain when students are most observably engaged in the lesson.

The data provided by these three methods would be rich. As a researcher, you could identify trends more confidently than if you had used only one data-collection method. In addition, the data you collect first, with one method, can help shape the focus of the data you collect next, with other methods. For example, the responses from a survey of a large population could generate the focus questions for follow-up interviews of a target group.

In all cases, we adhere to the principle that well-planned, deliberate, and structured steps are better than a flurry of activity when it comes to data collection. Rich data come from thoughtful process, not from "busy" process. In Jim's recent research on the attributes of leadership in effective elementary schools (Parsons & Beauchamp, 2011), the research study hinged on only two key questions: "(1) What makes this school a good place for teaching and learning? and (2) How does your administration help make it so?" (p. 30). These two simple questions opened the door to a wealth of reflection and insight from the research participants.

We also know a person who, whenever she begins a meeting, asks people to write down answers to two simple questions with a sentence-long explanation. She is always researching, a little bit at a time, and her data, collected with this simple, quick process, has proved revealing.

Keeping track of data as you collect it

We are about to dive into the details of data collection. Before we do that, we want to encourage you to keep track of what you collect and your thoughts about it, as you collect it.

To outsiders and newcomers, doing research can be scary. To those who do not live with research every day, dealing with data seems esoteric and perhaps even a bit majestic—like what Jim expected when he asked for help to make a decision.

> I remember being faced with a critical life decision that involved the opportunity to move to a new job. If I took it, I would be teaching at a seminary—which is something I really wanted to do—rather than at a public university. The job was far from Edmonton and meant uprooting my children, and so on. To help make my decision, I went to the most spiritually, guru-ish person I knew and asked him for divine insight.
>
> He listened and said, "Draw a line down a sheet of paper. On one side, put the positives; on the other, put the negatives. Then measure them. Which list is longer?" This was not what I wanted. I wanted some direct tap on the mind of the Creator. Some hocus-pocus stuff with smoke and candles, I guess. I was disappointed. God should reveal Herself in greater majesty than through a line down a piece of paper.

Handling data is less like something you don't know how to do, and more like drawing a line down a sheet of paper.

That said, the systematic tracking of the data is one of the most difficult areas of research to get your head around without experience. Experience—the one commodity you may not have in abundance—is a good teacher. But if you have never been taught by experience, then what?

One way to overcome a lack of experience is to learn from the techniques of those who do research for a living. Full-time researchers know their craft and have developed systems for their work. A classic research article by Miles and Huberman discussed, as far back as 1984, some simple ways researchers can keep track of data as they collect it. The authors call these methods of keeping up *interim data reduction techniques.*

The real task of research is to create sound from noise. In other words, as a researcher you enter a dynamic world of buzzing activity. Without a way to order this activity into something that makes sense, it is impossible to understand what is going on. We believe you should draw lines down the centres of papers. In other words, the data-handling techniques that work best are usually the most simple. They are also the most systematic and the easiest to attend to regularly.

Like most good research techniques, the ways Miles and Huberman (1984) "reduce" data to meaningful "knowledge" are actually quite simple.

Contact summary sheets are summaries of interviews or site visits on a single sheet of paper with information about the people and events, main themes, issues, the research questions addressed, new hypotheses, speculations, and target issues for the next interview or visit.

Coded data sheets are descriptive/high-inference checklists that look for patterns of behaviour. There are many of these available, or you may make up your own—depending on what you are looking for. The key here is to come up with systematic descriptors or keywords for the behaviours or incidences that you observe.

Memos are brief conceptual looks at an insight, a puzzle, a surprise, an emerging explanation, a striking event, or something similar that you notice in your data. It's sort of like keeping a notepad on the table near your bed. When something comes to you, write it down. (You will find that you will be constantly thinking about your research in your off-hours. You don't have to put your life on hold, but when an insight occurs to you, get in the habit of writing it down.)

We once worked with a teacher who wrote long e-mails spelling out the difficulties of understanding her data. Our reaction was to collect and save these e-mails, and send them back when it came time for her to write about the work. These e-mails became an excellent set of examples that highlighted the work. The teacher had, without even realizing it, written memos throughout the project.

Interim summaries are short, provisional syntheses of what the researcher knows to date (they may include a review of findings, a check of the robustness of supporting data, and so on). Every once in a while—say, on Saturday morning with a coffee—stop and write. Make notes about what has occurred to you at that moment. If possible, share your notes with a critical friend and ask for her feedback.

Important: save your work!
Remember to save all your work for later use. Have a special place on your computer or in a notebook for your data tracking. Eventually it adds up. You will be surprised, when the time comes, how much you actually have done.

Collecting data with surveys
Entire books are written on the topic of creating workable surveys. For your research, we hope the brief introduction that follows will provide some guidance, if you have not written a survey before. Writing good surveys is both an art and a science. The art (or instinct) lies in asking the types of questions that genuinely engage the interests and concerns of your participants. The science lies in structuring a survey to get the information you want in ways you can somehow measure.

Common survey woes
Make sure the data you collect actually help your research. This statement may seem obvious, but you would be amazed at how often

surveys generate results that no one can use. There are several reasons why surveys sometimes don't work.

The first reason is that participants can answer in surprising ways. If your question is vague, you might get answers you cannot classify consistently. For example, suppose you ask the question "What is your favourite class?" You want to know what students view as their favourite class in *school*, but because you weren't specific enough, some respondents may list a class that they were involved in *outside of school*, such as karate or candle making.

A second reason surveys can go astray is that you need to think and work somewhat backwards. Start with your final destination in mind: How will you use the data you gather? For example, a community league surveys some teenagers about their leisure interests so it can plan future spending. Participants are asked to check off facilities or leisure programs they would like to see in their area. When the researcher sits down to evaluate his survey results, he realizes he has no way to measure what choice was most desirable. In fact, some participants have checked off all the options he provided. Had he thought a little more carefully about how he would use his survey results, he probably would have asked participants to rank their choices from most to least desirable. A ranking would have provided more usable data.

A third common mistake is the failure to distinguish between preferences and intent. In the example above, many teens said they would "like" to have a skateboard park in their community. This tells the planners very little. Perhaps everyone would like a skateboard park (preference), but how many people would actually use it (intent)? If they did use it, how often would they use it? Participants will often support an idea on paper with no clear idea of how or even if they would be involved in its implementation. Measuring intent is crucially important.

Take time and expend effort to construct your survey. Ask for feedback before you distribute it. Have a colleague take your survey. You don't want the frustration of sitting with a stack of only semiuseful data after all the time and trouble you (and your participants) have gone through to gather it.

Finally, be careful with how you use language. In one huge international study, despite the year-long scrutiny of a host of learned researchers, a survey used the phrase "a couple of times" in questions when the better phrase might have been "one or two times." ("A couple" can be a purposely vague answer, like the answer drivers might give police when asked how many drinks they've had.) The response "one or two times" has a more specific, and thus more useful, meaning.

As we noted earlier, it is wise to have an outsider—meaning, *not* you—read your work and, if possible, actually take your survey. This is called a pilot test, and it helps you avoid mistakes that can haunt you for the entire life of your project. Always remember, it is better to take five minutes **now** to fix a problem than many hours **later** to cover a problem up. (The same is true, by the way, with citations in your review of literature.) Why are we saying this? Because we have had to pay for our research sins, and we want to help you avoid these same problems.

Closed-ended questions

Survey questions can have one of two basic structures: closed-ended and open-ended. Each has advantages and disadvantages that should be considered.

Closed-ended questions restrict the participant to a range of responses that you, as researcher, have made available. They are most useful when you need to measure (quantify) the data you gather and use it to generate statistics. You will no doubt recognize, in the examples that follow, types of questions you have encountered in surveys you have taken yourself.

List questions provide a number of items or statements, usually accompanied by some sort of checkbox. Participants may be asked to select as many items as apply, or to rank the items on the list in order of importance.

1. Recently, the board of directors for Blacksmith Academy discussed suggestions for increasing enrolment. In your opinion, which of these suggestions should the board pursue further? Check as many as apply.

   - tuition caps
   - targeting older students
   - charm school for instructors
   - presentations at high schools
   - improving practicum program
   - promoting scholarships available
   - daycare program for students with children

2. Blacksmith Academy is considering standardizing its final exams for all students. In your opinion, which of the following formats is most appropriate? Please rank your responses from 1 to 5, writing "1" next to the most appropriate, "2" next to the second most appropriate, and so on.

   - essay exam
   - practical exam
   - oral exam

- short-answer/multiple-choice exam
- no final exam: evaluate a year-end portfolio

Exclusive categories ask participants to select one and only one category into which they fit. Common examples are questions that ask you to select the age range or income range you fit into.

What is your annual income? (Check the income range that applies to you.)

- $10,000 or less
- $10,001–$24,999
- $25,000–$49,999
- $50,000–$89,999
- $90,000 or more

Likert scale–type questions are usually used to survey beliefs, perceptions, and attitudes. These questions give you a continuum with, for example, "very satisfied" at one end and "very dissatisfied" at the other end.

(Check one category). I kiss my children goodnight:

- Always (every day)
- Often (3–4 times a week)
- Sometimes (1–2 times a week)
- Rarely (less frequently than once a week)

Closed-ended questions have one major disadvantage: they provide no opportunity for participants to identify their own issues and concerns. Say, for instance, that you ask your research participants to rank the "top five things that make you upset at work" from a list you've provided. On your list you've included: dirty washrooms, inadequate air conditioning, and when the copier runs out of toner. Yet the biggest problem the staff have at this organization (and the one you did **not** include on your list) is the incessant elevator music piped into the office. Your participants cannot tell you because this important issue is not an item on your checklist.

One way to help work around this problem is to create an "other" category and ask participants to explain what their "other" is. Although responses might not be consistent from participant to participant, this addition can help you catch things you might have missed. In fact, you can always combine closed-ended questions and open-ended questions. Here's an example of two possible questions to add to a survey otherwise composed of closed-ended questions:

After filling out the survey, do you feel that any important questions were missed? If so, tell us what the survey failed to have you answer.
In assessing your school, what does an insider know that an outsider should know but cannot?

Open-ended questions

The problem we've just described suggests that it is generally wise to include open-ended questions in your survey. These invite your participants to respond in a more in-depth and individualized manner. Open-ended questions ask "How?" "Why?" and "In what ways?" These encourage thoughtful responses. Avoid questions that prompt yes/no or single-word answers.

For example, here are two versions of the same question with answers they might generate.

Closed-ended structure
Q Has the department been helpful to you in the past six months?
A No, not really.

Open-ended structure
Q In what ways have you found this department helpful during the past six months? Please describe any experiences with this department (positive or negative) in detail.
A The department hasn't been very helpful to me. When I phone for information, they often don't return my calls.

Although open-ended questions are intended to provide your participants with more latitude in their responses, you may still need to be directive. Sometimes people need some prompting or some triggers to recall important information. In other words, be specific enough that you are still targeting the information you really need.

In the following example, a question seeking information about staff areas inside a school gets off-target responses because the term *facilities* is vague.

Vague
Q What problems have you had with the school's facilities for staff in the past six months?
A Delivery trucks sometimes block my parking space.

Specific
Q In what way(s) could we improve the coffee area for staff?
A Furniture would be nice.
Q In what way(s) could we improve the library/research area for staff?
A Move the book stacks by the window farther apart. They are hard to access.

Open-ended questions have disadvantages, however. First, as you've probably guessed, responses can be highly individualized and thus difficult to classify or categorize. While site-based research lends itself well to the qualitative data gathered in open-ended questions, there may still be areas where you want measurable, consistent responses. In these cases, do not use open-ended questions.

Also, you can burn out participants with a long survey of open-ended questions, which require more time and effort to fill out. If you overload participants with questions that require lengthy responses, the quality (and quantity) of these responses is likely to go down. By page three, you'll be noticing two- or three-word responses, and questions that haven't been answered at all. Limit the number of open-ended questions you use. You might also break it up a bit by interspersing open-ended and closed-ended questions.

Tips for writing surveys

- Write in language that your participants can easily understand. Keep it simple.
- Define any terms your participants may be unfamiliar with. Avoid jargon.
- In the introduction, explain the survey's purpose. Give participants an idea of how long it will take to complete (as a general rule, 10 minutes or less is a timeframe to aim for).
- Ask one question at a time. Even in a series of related questions, it is best to create one response item per question.
- Plan in advance how you will use the information you've gathered.
- Test your survey, or review it with a critical friend or small pilot group, before mass circulation.
- Consider the following questions: Does the survey make sense? Is it easy to fill out? Is all the information useful and relevant?
- Frame sensitive questions carefully. Even anonymous participants can be touchy about admitting to negative thoughts, feelings, or behaviours.
- Consider later disaggregation needs (e.g., separating male from female responses). Ask for this relevant information at the top of the survey.
- Remember to thank participants for their time.

Collecting data with interviews

Surveys are useful tools for quickly and consistently collecting data to help your project. However, the trade-off for this efficient breadth of data might be a loss of depth in responses. For this reason, researchers often find it worthwhile to supplement the information they gather from surveys with the more detailed, nuanced, and often more personal insights that can be gathered from interviews. Jones (1985) reminds us of the power of engaging in dialogue:

> to understand other persons' constructions of reality, we would do well to ask them...and to ask them in such a way that they can tell us in their terms (rather than those imposed rigidly and a priori by ourselves)

and in a depth which addresses the rich context that is the substance of their meanings. (p. 46)

Interviews allow this rich dialogue to add substantial depth to your research data.

Choosing an interview structure

Interviews may be as structured or unstructured as you would like them to be (to learn more about structured, semistructured, and unstructured interviewing, see Fontana and Frey, 1994). The important points to consider (as always when gathering data) are the practical constraints of your research (you might not have time to learn every subject's life story) and how you are planning to use the information you gather. Consider the information in Table 3, which summarizes key differences between interview formats with more and less structure, as you make these decisions.

LESS STRUCTURE: AN EMERGENT INTERVIEW

A researcher might be gathering historical information about an organization. He is only looking for a feel about what has been done in the past and will look for themes later when he reviews his data. Also, the people he is interviewing come from a wide variety of backgrounds within the organization and have served in different capacities for different lengths of time through different eras of

Table 3. COMPARING INTERVIEW FORMATS

MORE STRUCTURE	LESS STRUCTURE
Responses are: • more consistent • easier to code and analyze • less rich	Responses are: • less consistent, because interview contents may vary considerably • more difficult to code and analyze • more rich
The interviewer: • aims to be more impartial • has more control over the shape and direction of the interview • needs less experience to be successful	The interviewer: • has more opportunity to build a trusting relationship with participants • has more opportunity to encounter and explore ideas and insights initiated by the research subject • needs good interviewing skills, strong people skills
The interview: • is generally more formal • is potentially more efficient and less time-consuming	The interview: • can be more conversational • can be more time-consuming

the organization. In this case, an unstructured interview would be appropriate.

MORE STRUCTURE: A SEMISTRUCTURED INTERVIEW

Say, for instance, you want to investigate the learning experiences of teachers who attended a recent all-day team-building workshop. One of your goals is to document how different people can have widely varying perceptions of the same events. Here you are able to use a fairly structured interview format because all your interviewees attended the same workshop. This format also helps you to capture and compare different perceptions. In a semistructured interview, the researcher uses standardized questions in a standardized order; zero follow-up questions; and precoded categories to record responses. In essence, the format minimizes flexibility and variation, with the interviewer playing an impartial role.

If you choose a more structured format, you can provide participants with an advance list of your questions. The list sets the framework for the interview and allows participants to think ahead—if they choose—in preparation for the conversation. Participants are also fully informed about what to expect, which can help put them at ease in the interview. They are able to make an informed decision about doing the interview. (Providing this choice is fundamental to ethical research.)

An example of interview questions: mentorship models

This example comes from a research project that explored possible mentorship models for the YMCA. This researcher accompanied her list of questions with a preinterview written survey, thus combining some qualitative and some quantitative data in her study.

Dear Participant:

Thank you for your interest in participating. The following list of questions will be used to guide our conversation during your personal interview. Do not fill in either Part 1 or Part 2 of this form, as notes will be taken for you. However, it may help to jot down your thoughts and ideas on a separate sheet of paper.

Interview questions
1. What is your job/position at the YMCA?
2. What do you like about working at the YMCA?
3. What don't you like about working at the YMCA?
4. What concerns do you have regarding your workplace environment?
5. Do you know why employees have quit?

6. How do you think retention can be improved? Why? What needs to change?
7. Based on your experiences being part of a self-directed team, give an example of a challenge the team had. Describe the challenge and how the team responded.
8. Describe a situation in which you were able to build a relationship with a member of management, even when you felt the situation was difficult.
9. What is your perception of the management's mentorship effectiveness?

Conducting an interview

When conducting an interview, pay careful consideration to how you can set your participant at ease. In addition to taking time to ensure a pleasant interview area (comfortable chair, water, etc.), the rapport you establish can help you collect more meaningful information. Reviewing with the participant the project and the procedures for the interview are great first steps. Remember, participants have given up their time to talk to you.

You will also need to consider how to collect information during the interview. Are you asking questions and taking notes? Do you have an assistant or colleague able to take written notes for you? Are you using audio or video recording equipment to allow for later review? Carefully considering how you will collect the data given by your participants can save later agony, as you put your memory to the test to recall the specific phraseology used by participants in particular responses.

Tips for conducting interviews

- Set a timeframe, but not a stringent one.
- Be prepared. Have your recording equipment (if using any) and other needed materials ready. Practise your interview with a colleague or friend, asking for feedback to help improve the interview experience for your participants.
- Offer participants a preview of interview questions and a general outline of the process to be followed.
- Enable participants to elaborate as a way to enrich the conversation and the results.
- Note your observations about body language if it impacts the study.
- Keep your personal feelings and opinions at bay to avoid biasing the data.
- People are glad to help. However, give them the opportunity to stop or to say no at any time, and respect their choice.

- The location of the interview is important. Choose a quiet location.
- Set up the interview well in advance, with times and dates. This will allow participants to prepare and to make room in their schedules.

Collecting data with focus groups

Like interviews, focus groups involve face-to-face interactions—this time, however, with groups of subjects rather than a single subject. This adds some extra dimensions to the method of data collection.

In one-on-one interviews, the privacy of the information shared is relatively straightforward—it is easy to manage the data shared because only you and your research subject know what was said in the interview. The case is quite different in a focus group. Here all participants witness one another's perspectives on the research questions. And, the more sensitive the topic, the more thought and care are required to manage the process (the event itself) and the information that emerges from it (your data).

It is important, then, to take a strong leadership role in the facilitation of your focus group by clearly explaining the ground rules for group conduct and the nature of the information shared. It is up to you to establish a constructive discussion in a respectful atmosphere. In a number of ways, this process resembles developing team norms when working in collaborative groups. Consider the steps you will need to create a safe environment for your participants and how much time you will need to prepare.

Some guidelines for focus groups

- Consider what information you can share with participants—perhaps in an e-mail or a letter—before the event to better prepare them for the experience.
- Consider scripting your opening comments to ensure clear communication of expectations and procedures. Have a colleague or coresearcher review your script to identify areas that are not clear or need further explanation.
- Think of your first question as an icebreaker. Which of your research questions would be best?
- Explain ground rules explicitly (perhaps with a preliminary meeting), and be prepared for people to leave if they cannot adhere to the group rules.
- Stress the need for confidentiality and anonymity: what is said in the room stays in the room.
- Offer participants an opportunity to add to ground rules.

ENGAGING IN ACTION RESEARCH

- Be considerate of tone, terminology, and organizational culture.
- Consider the topic's sensitivity. Participants are sharing with others, not just you.
- If the discussion is stressful, how do the participants feel once they have left the group? Be sensitive to the possible need for debriefing.
- Create a safe environment for participants: avoid settings of conflict or hierarchy.
- If using a recording device, obtain permission to record from all participants in advance of the focus-group session, if possible. Otherwise, clearly explain how the data will be recorded and used.
- Don't push too hard: if a participant is holding back despite your encouragement, there is probably a good reason.
- Be prepared to be surprised, and remain flexible.

Obtaining authentic and trustworthy data from focus groups

- Develop questions using a vocabulary appropriate for your participants.
- Explain how the focus-group data will be used.
- Immediately after the focus group, build in time to synthesize the group's perceptions. Begin the process of looking at themes to share with participants, and verify and validate the content.
- Compare the themes that emerge from your focus group with what you have learned from your literature review and any other data collection you may have done (triangulation).
- Use multiple groups with different individuals on the same topic.
- Create a relaxed atmosphere of psychological safety, group support, and personal openness—an informal, nonjudgmental environment motivates simple and direct communication.
- Participants will build on each other's responses. Predetermine useful prompts to draw out information.

Choosing focus-group participants

A provincial organization we know recently had a negative focus-group experience. Twenty participants were brought together to discuss the effectiveness with which a project, involving partner organizations, had been carried out. This undertaking was politically sensitive to begin with, never mind that some participating organizations (which had not been represented in the focus group) were soundly slammed in the report that emerged from this event.

The written results of the focus group barely saw daylight. Critics within the offended organizations correctly charged that the focus-group participants—drawn informally and on a volunteer basis by word of mouth—were hardly a fair sampling of project stakeholders. And, if they were volunteering for the group, what axes did the participants have to grind or what personal agendas did they have to promote? Further, why were some partner organizations unaware that the focus group had even taken place? The report literally wound up in the shredder, special arrangements needed to be made to apologize to the partner organizations, and dismissals ensued.

There is a lesson here: poor work can and does happen in the real world, and it leads to poor research and suspect findings. Take care that ethical and professional protocols guide your work with focus groups.

- Ensure that all interested parties have an opportunity to participate.
- Communicate the intent of the focus group.
- Use a rigorous selection process that you can describe and defend.
- Ensure that participants represent multiple points of view.
- Do not use research as a hammer to clobber others into shape.

Focus-group participants should be selected with care and sensitivity. For example, if you know some participants well, how might this affect the dynamics of the group? Will staff members feel they can be completely open and honest in front of administrators? Do some participants have agendas or biases that might influence their contributions? Will participants fairly represent others in their cohort? Do participants form a balanced representation of important stakeholders in your research issue? All these questions bear scrutiny as you develop your focus group. The trustworthiness of your data is only as good as the participants who provide it.

Tips for conducting focus groups

We give you a lot of tips in this section. Here are a few more, on the practical side.

- Be sure your technology works. For example, is the audio recording device functioning properly? Will background noise drown out participant voices?
- Plan for at least two "staff" people (including you)—one to facilitate and one to record/observe. A third person could observe a particular aspect of the group—for example, focusing solely on participants' body language. Be sure to arrange back-ups for these people, in case of illness or unexpected absence.

- Provide food and beverages for participants.
- Know in advance the topics you want to discuss. Test your open-ended questions beforehand to determine if you will get the kind of information you want to collect.
- Take time to prepare the space. Is the room temperature comfortable? Lighting? Seating?
- Have name tags for participants, and allow them to write in their own names.
- Ask participants to identify themselves before they speak.
- Have extras of essential items ready: paper, pencils, refreshments.

Open-space research

Open-space research—or "open space" for short—can be viewed as a type of focus-group research. It is a large-group technique that works well when the input of many stakeholders is desired. Bryson and Anderson (2000) describe its aim as seeking information from as many members of an organization as possible. Open space is often structured as a data-collection "event." The event starts as a large group, and then breaks out into self-organized smaller groups that discuss particular topics. The smaller groups run as concurrent sessions, either in parts of a larger room, or in separate rooms.

Characteristics of open-space research

According to Harrison Owen (1997, p. 41), open space operates on four key principles that maximize the impact of the participants. Research participants are informed of these simple principles:

- Whoever comes are the right people.
- Whatever happens is the only thing that could have happened.
- Whenever it starts is the right time.
- When it's over, it's over.

Owen further articulates the following ground rules for open space, which work well in our experience:

- All issues of concern to all in attendance will be raised.
- All issues raised will be discussed to the extent desired.
- All participants will receive a written report on the proceedings of the event by the end of the event.
- Participants will determine priorities and prepare results-orientated action plans.
- Using the law of "two feet," participants can move to any other small-group discussion anytime they become uninterested, have finished contributing, or simply wish to move on.

How to create an open-space research event

Running an open-space event is similar in many ways to running a focus group. Some of the same basics apply, such as: making sure you discuss issues of confidentiality and security with your participants; describing to participants the ways that you will use the data; making sure your equipment is available and working before the session.

The large number of participants, and the end-of-day report on proceedings, add some additional steps.

- Make sure the people you need at the session—the people who have the information that answers your research questions—know about the event. Send them an invitation that outlines the purpose of the event, the date, time, place, focus, and a description of the process.
- Set up a registration process for participants, both in advance of the event and on the day.
- Make sure your location is big enough for the number of participants you anticipate.
- Make sure you have separate people to do these jobs: (1) facilitate the event, (2) collate the report on proceedings for the end of the event.
- Prepare copies of a consent form, one for each participant.
- It will be a large group. Consider if you need handouts for any part of the process. Consider whether you need flipcharts or other ways for the break-out groups to work through their discussions.
- You need to generate a report on proceedings by the end of the event. A good way is to arrange for each break-out group to have a laptop. (In the invitation to the event, you could ask participants to bring their own laptops, or you could recruit "recording secretaries" from your lucky friends and family). Make sure you have access to printers and photocopiers.
- Create a process that allows participants to remove their input from the data, if they so choose. It's unlikely this will happen much, but the process could be for participants to inform the facilitator, who would then inform the person collating the proceedings.

Holding your open-space event

- On the day of the event, set up the chairs in the space in a large circle. Ensure inclusivity for all participants.
- Introduce and welcome participants to the event and state the overall purpose of the research. Talk about what you hope to

accomplish during the event; security and privacy procedures; and how you will use the data you collect.

- Ask each participant to complete the consent form.
- Take questions.
- "Open the space" by stating the principles and ground rules of open-space research. State the research question.
- Ask the group to generate topics for discussion that relate to the research question. Record these in a way that allows the whole group to see them.
- Assign a location for the discussion of each topic. If you have many topics, you may need to run more than one set of concurrent break-out groups. Consider this, and then assign a time limit for the break-out groups (e.g., one hour for the first set of groups discussing topics 1 through 6; one hour for the second set of groups discussing topics 7 through 12).
- Ask the participants to disperse to the break-out group of their choice. Remind participants that they do not have to stay in a group if it is not interesting to them or if they want to experience a number of groups. Unless you have recruited recording secretaries, ask each group to appoint someone who will stay with the group and create a record of who attended, key topics, and preliminary recommendations.
- To "close the space," ask all participants to return to the large group. Ask each person to comment on his or her experience in the space, and share priorities that arose from discussions. For the purposes of data collection, make sure to record in some detail what the participants say. This can be a powerful part of the event—often a great deal of information and emotion grows from this sharing of experiences and perspectives.
- While this final large-group discussion is going on, collate the proceedings from the small-group discussions.
- In a preliminary way, describe the insights you, as a researcher, collected from the event. If appropriate, ask for volunteers to help steer next steps, such as actions or further discussions arising from the event.
- Give each participant a copy of the small-group proceedings. Send a final corrected and formatted copy to all participants as soon as possible, and include information from the final large-group discussion, as well as any decisions on actions or further discussions.

Collecting data through observation

We think observation is perhaps the most fun—and in many ways the most informative—aspect of research. It is people-watching with a research purpose. On the downside, observation can be time-consuming. Perhaps you will not spend the sort of time Jane Goodall did with her apes. (When her institute wrote the book *Forty Years at Gombe: A Tribute to Four Decades of Wildlife Research, Education, and Conservation*, they really meant 40 years.) Still, it takes time to do observation well. It is seldom possible to get a feel for a situation after only one or two observation sessions.

Even if observation is not your main research method, it can play an important part, and you should work to create some "formal" ways to note your observations (such as forms or templates you can use in a practical manner). Creating forms for keeping track of your research is an idea we will keep repeating. Many researchers keep personal journals during their research projects, and observations can be recorded in these journals simply as a way of building insight and context for the study. Some simply spend an hour with coffee each Saturday morning to reflect on the past week, keeping an unedited log of activities on their computer.

Or you may decide that observation will form part of your research method or plan, in which case you will need to be careful, systematic, and rigorous about what and how you record. But, however you use observation, it will enrich your work. The following information should help you hone your watching and listening skills.

Study the research setting using all your senses

When real estate agents hold open houses, they often suggest that their sellers burn candles or bake bread to make the house smell good. Interior designers may pore over colour charts choosing a look for a corporate office that suggests it is eco-friendly. A restaurant's atmosphere—if it has unpleasant odors, an appearance of uncleanliness, and a suspicious lack of other customers—might make you want to turn and walk out the door. We use information from our senses to respond to environments, and we study these environments to help us form impressions of the kinds of people who hang out there. A rich description of the physical space where your observations are taking place can lend insight about the people who occupy that space.

Don't forget, too, that the timing of your observations is an important aspect of your setting. Superintendents will tell you that observations conducted in September will yield very different experiences than those conducted in June. Another example: any teacher will tell you that the class first thing in the morning is *very* different from the class just before lunch!

Study the research participants

Researchers often work best from structure. The following questions provide a way to organize your insights. If you can answer these questions, you might then develop a systematic way to gain insight into the people who are your participants. Many of these questions might dig too deep and not fit your research needs, but they give you a sense of what you might look for.

- Does the person's physical appearance tell you anything? Do any of these appearances reflect organizational culture? (Watch for posture, movements, dress, and physical features.)
- Does the person use esoteric or organizational language, or uncommon expressions of speech? Does the organization have a vocabulary—particular ways of saying things?
- Does the person behave (have habits or special interests) in ways that reflect organizational thinking?
- What makes this person special, and is this specialness related to the organization in which the person lives and works? Why does this person stand out from the crowd?
- What physical evidence can you find that tells you something about the person or the organization? (Think like an anthropologist or archaeologist. Don't forget photos, collections of items, things on desks, or magazines lying around.)

Separate observations from judgments and inferences

An old maxim for writers is "show, don't tell." This maxim means that it is better to demonstrate something—and let readers draw their own insights—than to tell readers what to think. Here is a simple example that gives two versions of the same situation.

Version 1
The student was upset by an incident that happened at recess.

Version 2
The student was pale and shaking after returning to his seat following recess. He was smiling and talkative earlier that day, but I now found him uncommunicative. I entered the classroom three times that afternoon to invite him to talk, but he was not willing to share for the remainder of the day.

We believe the second version does a better job. In the first version, we are left to ask (1) how the observer knew the student was upset and (2) how the observer came to the certainty that it was a recess incident that had caused this condition. The second version spells out the circumstances and the results. Better writing reveals more about research situations and is more interesting to read.

The second version describes—with good detail—what the observer observed. It does not make assumptions about the *meaning* of what was observed; that is left for future analysis. Suppose, for instance, that after several more interactions with this student, the researcher in question begins to believe that the student is becoming increasingly more despondent as the end of the day approaches. In this case, the possibility that a recess incident was to blame is less certain. Yet in the first version, this possibility is stated as a certainty—as a fact. Remember, once you write something in a categorical manner—as if there were no other choice—you must take responsibility for what you have written. It is difficult to go back and remember, or rework, your insights.

We hope this example illustrates the danger of making too many early assumptions about what you are observing. We encourage you to be conscious that making observations—what you can see, touch, or hear—is a separate process from *inferring* or judging what those observations mean.

To get around this potential problem, you can make a point of separating your observations from your judgments in your notes. Create two columns on your sheet of paper or in your document. On the left side, note your empirical observations (i.e., what you can experience with your senses). On the right, note your own reflections, questions, or thoughts about what your observations mean. Social studies teachers use a strategy called "clue and conclusion" to extract results from documents and photographs that may provide a deeper understanding to a topic. We "see" clues through observation, but we make conclusions based on those clues.

OBSERVATION	REFLECTIONS/NOTES
Tess physically withdrew as the math class progressed. She closed her book early, became increasingly more distracted by others around her, and played with items in her desk at one point for approximately 4 uninterrupted minutes.	Is Tess having trouble with the math content? She seems to pay attention during teacher instruction but disengages when needing to work on the content individually. Or is it difficulty staying attentive when working independently? I wonder what she is like in other subject areas.

ENGAGING IN ACTION RESEARCH

Tips for observing as a researcher

Glesne and Peshkin (1992) offer many useful insights on how to observe. In our own research, we have found these procedures work well:

- Study the setting using all your senses. Use descriptive words to document your perceptions.

- If you are looking within your own organization, try to *make the familiar strange*. Imagine yourself as a complete newcomer to this setting, and take a fresh look at all of those subtle "background elements" you've probably come to take for granted.

- For each thing you notice, ask "Does this mean something?"

- Study your participants. Ask and answer questions that reveal both the person and the organization in which the person "lives." Who are they in terms of age, gender, social class, and ethnicity? How are they dressed? How do they interact? What do they talk about?

- Study the events. Differentiate between special events and common daily events. Look for the subtle little acts that make up each event.

- Study people's gestures. How do people show attitude and emotion? What gestures are used? Why?

- Focus on behaviours and concrete details. These are easier to work with later when you want to start working your field notes into categories for analysis.

Collecting data through document analysis

Document analysis involves examining the content and structure of documents as a way to gain insight into their meaning for those who engage them and who are engaged by them.

"Documents" can be any number of things—for example, photographs, tools, or written information such as books or school-vision statements. Almost certainly, you will find documents that will help answer your research questions. Sometimes these documents might hold unique importance for your research; sometimes they provide a way to gain further insight into data you have collected with other methods.

As with any data-collection method, effective document analysis must have a firm grounding in your research questions and project goals. Keep your focus. Be selective. Engage what *counts*, not *everything*.

- Consider the sort of documents that might contain what you are seeking. What documents hold promise in your study? What information are you seeking in these documents? How many different documents will you study?

- Outline the context and environment in which these documents exist. Why and for what purpose were these documents created? Who created them?

- Define the features you care about. What, specifically, are you looking for? What relationships can you identify between your document study and the questions of the larger research project?
- Study these features. What are you seeing as you examine the documents you have chosen? What redundancies do you see? What stands out as odd? What sense do you get about what the creators of these documents see as important? What do the creators reveal about their interests?
- Take wide notes as you review each document. Although you might not use all the notes you take, these wide notes will help you find the broadest interpretation of the document in your analysis.

Marshalling your participants

Except for document analysis, all the data-collection methods we have covered in this chapter require participants. To conclude the chapter, we offer some pointers on how to contact participants for your research with examples of cover letters and a consent form. These pointers, like all our tips, come from a number of years of work, and we hope they will save you time and energy.

Regardless of the method you choose—surveys, interviews, focus groups, or observation—it is necessary to write a cover letter that provides as much information as possible to your potential participants. A cover letter is a practical consideration that ensures participants' questions are answered consistently and in advance of the research. A cover letter has two advantages: first, it saves you time because you are not answering and reanswering many of these questions in your scheduled session; second, it's ethical to inform your participants as much as possible of your research intentions. Your advance notice can also put your subjects at ease; they will know exactly what they can expect.

The example cover letters we have here are for interviews with organizations and individuals. In either case, the letter informs your research participants of:

- your credentials and your reasons for doing the site-based research project
- the purpose and topic of your study and why the individual's or organization's input would be valued
- the general format of the interview or survey you will be conducting (length of time required, types of questions that will be asked)

- any other information that your subjects might need for preparation

More specifically and at the time of the interview or survey, you should have participants sign a consent form that outlines the conditions under which the research will take place. For both yourself as researcher and your participants, your consent form needs to outline rights, responsibilities, and obligations.

If you are working with children as participants, you need to address your cover letter to the parents of the children, and (just like for school outings), you need parents' permission for the participation of their children in advance of your research (before the day).

Example of a cover letter to an organization

October 10, 2012

H. Davidson, VP Public Relations
Re: "Best case practices" for attracting and retaining short-term teachers

Dear Mr. Davidson,

Thank you for agreeing to meet with me regarding the "best case practices" interview. As you are aware, your school has been identified as having successful teacher-employment practices. This letter provides you with background information prior to our meeting and also shares the interview questions.

My name is Cade McCale, and I am a university student from the University of Alberta. I am conducting a study on best practices for retaining teachers. This study is in partial fulfillment of the requirements for the Master of Education degree I am pursuing at the University of Alberta. As part of the study, I am collecting information from schools with a successful history of teacher employment.

The interview will take approximately one hour. All identifiable responses will be kept anonymous and confidential, and will be used in a best-practices final report as one part of a research project. I will be the only person with access to any identifiable individual responses, in order to analyze data for the final study report.

I anticipate that a final report for this project will be available by the end of May 2013. A copy of the final report will be available to view at your request. Participation in this research is voluntary, and you may withdraw at any time.

If you have any questions, please call me at (250) 250–2222 or e-mail cmcale@house.com. Your time and input would be greatly appreciated. Thank you in advance for your consideration.

Sincerely,
Cade McCale

Example of a cover letter to an individual participant.

October 3, 2012

Dear Potential Research Participant,

You are invited, on a purely voluntary basis, to participate in a research study that investigates how collaborative, project-based teaching systemically affects student achievement.

I am conducting this study in partial fulfilment of the requirements for a Masters of Education degree from the University of Alberta. The information gathered from this survey will be used in combination with other data to identify the holistic effect on student learning of project-based teaching. The knowledge gained from this study will be provided to undergraduate teacher candidates at the University of Alberta as an aid to curriculum planning in their preservice education program.

Your opinions are important for this study. I hope to gain insight into ways our preservice instruction might be improved.

Your participation is completely voluntary, and you need only answer those questions you feel comfortable addressing. This survey is expected to take approximately fifteen minutes. All responses will be kept completely anonymous and strictly confidential. Only I, as the researcher, will have access to the individual responses to analyze data and prepare a final report. Dr. Jim Parsons from the University of Alberta is my academic advisor, and I can provide you with details, if you wish, to contact him regarding this study.

If you wish to receive information on the findings, I will gladly make them available to you once the study is complete. Data gathered will be kept in a locked filing cabinet for five years under the possibility that the data might be used for further research. After five years, all information in hard copy will be shredded and any electronic data will be destroyed.

By completing this survey, it is understood that you have read the above information and are freely consenting to participate in the study. If you have any questions, please contact me at 1–222–222–1978 (weekends) or 1–222–222–5225 (workweek) or via the e-mail address provided below.

By Tuesday, please seal your completed survey in the self-addressed envelope provided and return it to me, or send the completed survey by e-mail to wyatt.hurtzburg@holyspirits.ca. Your support in this research initiative is greatly appreciated, and I thank you for your time, input, and effort in this endeavour.

Sincerely,
Wyatt Hurtzburg
University of Alberta

Example of a research participant consent form

Research project: "Best case practices" for teacher employment
Researcher: Cade McCale, MEd Candidate (Master of Education, Traditional Crafts, University of Alberta)
Project supervisor: Dr. Mick Jaguar

Dear Participant,

Please read the following carefully. Your signature below indicates that you consent to participate in the above-named study, which will follow the methods described below:

- The interview will take approximately one hour.
- All interview data and conversations will be kept strictly confidential unless otherwise advised.
- Your participation is voluntary and anonymous. You can withdraw at any time. The researcher is the only individual who will know of your participation.
- The interview will be recorded, and you will have the right to stop the recording at any point during the interview. If this happens, the transcripts will be destroyed and recording erased at that point.
- The researcher will personally transcribe the recording. Identifiable information, recordings, and transcripts will be kept locked and secure in the researcher's home and will be destroyed once the study is complete (May 2013). Interview transcripts will not contain the real names of participants. A code number will identify your data throughout the research notes.
- You will be given a copy of the transcripts to review, verify, and revise at your discretion.
- The data from your interview will be one part of a thesis and may also be used in other forms such as professional journals, always maintaining the same standards of confidentiality and anonymity.
- There will be no monetary compensation for participating.
- A summary of the study results will be made available to you at the end of the project (May 2013) upon request.

You should feel free to ask for clarification or new information throughout your participation in this study.

If you have further questions concerning this research, please feel free to contact Cade McCale collect at (250) 250–2222 or e-mail cmcale@house.com.

Participant (*please print name*) _____

Signature _____ Date _____

Researcher (*please print name*) ___CADE MCCALE_____

Signature _____ Date _____

9

Analyzing your data

ESSENTIAL QUESTIONS
How can you make sense of the data you have collected?

CHAPTER PURPOSE
To organize your data into usable forms
To interpret your data into research findings

It is not enough to simply collect data and then abandon the data for others to make sense of. First, you have to organize the data; second, you have to analyze the data. These processes may seem new but, honestly, you already have the skill set to complete this task. Organizing your data is not so different from working with a review of literature. If you have already done that, you will have a sense of how to shape the data that you have. So, now that you are up to your ears in data, what should you do?

Whacks and whacks of data...now what?

Let us begin simply. The first question is "What do data look like?" The answer, most simply, is that data generally take two forms—one is sound and the other is text. Generally, sound comes from recordings of interviews or conversations or meetings, and the first thing many researchers do is reshape this sound into text. Some might even send it to an outsider (a transcriber, for example) to create that text. (Remember, any time you use an outside person to work with your data, you should review confidentiality requirements with them. Most professionals understand the importance of research ethics, but you should take this precaution anyway.) However, there are options to working exclusively with data in text form. In fact, there may be good reason to leave recorded sound as sound, and to shape it in that form.

For example, if you are interviewing participants about a controversial organizational issue, the words used have a definitional meaning but they might also carry an inflected meaning. You have no doubt had conversations with people whose language has simply dripped with irony. In that case, the words alone do not tell you the entire story. Or, sometimes it is impossible or difficult for practical reasons—including time and money—to transcribe tapes.

Working with recorded data: audio or audiovisual

Over the years, Jim has encouraged some of his graduate students to leave recorded data in their sound format. His instruction is to listen to the recordings three times:

1. First, listen to all the recordings in as short a time as possible to corroborate the sense you had of what was happening as the recordings were made. While you listen, take notes about what themes or categories you should use to organize your work.
2. Then, listen to clarify your themes in your head and take notes that would help you explain these themes to your readers.
3. Finally, listen to find the direct quotes you want to use to highlight the meanings of your themes—these are the grounds for creating your theories for your work.

After you have completed these steps, go ahead and write up your work.

Working with textual data

Textual data might take a number of forms.

Analysis of pictures or drawings—for example, a study of school logos or icons, or the photos a school uses to highlight its programming—is usually in the form of notes. Specifically, as you study the icons or photos, you would write down thoughts and observations about what they mean. The text you generate becomes the data you will work to organize. At this point, you as the researcher are back to shaping words from textual responses into meaning.

Surveys, either closed-ended or open-ended, are rather easy to organize into meaning. Typically, if you give a 10-question survey to one hundred students in a school, the easiest way to organize the responses is to begin with a short introduction and then to list the questions, one at a time, and quantify the responses.

This would be as true with simple answers ("choose *a, b, c, d,* or *e*") as with more open-ended responses. Typically one section of your final report would simply count the responses (the *What?* of your research findings). Another section would focus on analyzing the responses (to say what the responses mean—the *So what?* of your research findings).

Transcribed interviews or conversations provide the researcher with large chunks of text to review. However, the process of shaping the meaning of these is only slightly different from Jim's three-step process we outlined for recorded data:

1. Read the transcripts through to see that you have your head around what was happening. (We encourage you to take notes right on the transcripts.)
2. Read the transcripts to discover themes or categories for shaping the data into meaning. (We often use different coloured high-lighters, matched to themes we have identified—one colour for each theme—and mark anything that seems to fit the themes as we read.)
3. Read the transcripts to choose examples for citing. (Don't be afraid to mark all over the transcripts as you read them. These jotted notes—spur-of-the-moment ideas that come to you—can be really insightful later.)

Notes may take several forms, including posters, journals, e-mails, memos, and so on. Again, you might reshape the notes—posters that are artifacts of a focus-group session, for example—into more work-able (size-wise, for example) units. However, the three-step process to organize the content for meaning still applies:

1. Read for general understanding.
2. Read for organizational shaping (categories or themes).
3. Read for specific examples that illustrate important points. (As always, we encourage you to engage the texts you are reading as you read them. Take notes about whatever comes to you.)

In so many ways, organizing data differs little from organizing the notes you took when you completed your literature review. At the point of work, the text looks the same. And at the point of shaping, the process is remarkably similar. The end result is also the same— you are arranging bits and pieces of text into units that make your research clear and meaningful to your readers.

Interpreting your findings: the *So what?*

The three-step process to organize your data for meaning gets at the *What?* of your study. *What* did you find when you searched? *What* insights did the participants provide for your work?

The next step is the *So what?* At this point, you are working to provide insight for those who are reading your work. You've probably made all sorts of observations and speculations as you've conducted your research. We hope you have made lots of notes to yourself about what you've seen and considered. You can now use these notes and reflections just like any of the other textual data we've already discussed.

Review your notes for overall impressions

Slot your thoughts (as best you can) into an organizing framework. We find this process works best when we have the notes beside us at a computer. As we enter our thoughts about what we have reviewed, we move the cursor up and down—working to place any note into a sequence that initially makes sense to us. We don't worry much about the final work now, because we know we will edit this work many times. What we worry more about is that we capture all our thoughts and ideas as we have them. The text will be all over the place, and will take several revisions—always adding insights as we revise. We simply don't worry about getting it into any final form. That form will take shape as we work through our ideas.

Draw out specific examples...you know the process!

Beyond this, it is difficult to provide a simple recipe for analyzing data. There is no special set of directions for this work, except to be systematic, organized, honest, considerate, and careful. Our best advice, based on our own experience, is to make sure you capture all the ideas you have as you have them—even if it seems your work becomes sloppy. We can also offer a second bit of advice. In our work, we have seen two sorts of errors: the first is overstating what your data show, and the second is understating what your data show. You can evaluate whether you have overstated or understated things as you work through the final version of your research report.

Overstating happens when the data do not support the analysis. Weak data may trigger extra verbiage: the researcher tries desperately to create insights that were neither present in, nor supported by, the findings. Biases of the researcher, either conscious or unconscious, can be another trigger—the verbiage comes from the difficulty of letting go of hegemonic perspectives that allow only a narrow, pre-determined translation of the data. These are reasons to consult colleagues as you undertake your research project. Simply stated, it helps to talk things through with a trusted colleague.

Perhaps a more common problem is a researcher who is too cautious. Sometimes the data "say" more than the researcher shows. It is understandable to be cautious, because the opposite problem—overanalysis—seems such a risk. Our suggestion is to be daring and humble at the same time. When you do offer an insight, try to point to the footprints (data) that show where to follow the trail. Explain how you came to the conclusions that you did. If you can do this, your insights should be relatively safe ones. Again, this is an area where a critical friend might be extremely helpful. Talk about what you have seen, and listen to the insights of others who also care to look at your work.

We encourage you to take time during your research project to track your thoughts and ideas, and to share them with others. In the last chapter, we encouraged you to take up some form of personal note taking, such as memos, contact summary sheets, or interim summaries. You could e-mail these from time to time to a network of critical friends. One of the best things about your school, division, or provincial research partners is that they become ready and willing friends. Organize your community for the mutual benefit of your own and their own work.

Interpreting data: Jim's steps
All researchers come to know their data better as they spend time with the data.

Jim, as part of his continuing research work at the University of Alberta, engages in regular research projects. Often these projects take place over a two- or three-year time span. The process is interesting because, after two or three years, the data become so real. You really get to know the data!

Jim's work is practical—he wants to know how to improve educational practice. He asks three basic questions about his data:

- What? (What did we find?)
- So what? (What do these findings mean?)
- Now what? (What should we do after we make sense of the findings?)

After spending so much time working to figure out what the data might mean to practice (working to answer these three questions), Jim comes to understand the data almost like it is second nature, and the data start to reveal insights.

So, spend the time to better understand your data.

E-mailing the stars
It might seem daring, but as you gain insights into your data, you can talk about them with other researchers.

During your literature review (and, we're guessing, your ongoing reading), you found interesting articles on research related to yours. It's worth remembering that somebody completed that research. Most of these researchers work for academic institutions and their e-mail addresses can be found. If you find a particularly cogent research project and decide to cite it, we encourage you to find the researchers who originally completed that research, and share your own insights and findings—and questions you might have. This is how knowledge gets shared among researchers. This process of e-mailing other authors is something Jim has practised for many years. Many long e-mail conversations have ensued that share work insights. And, in the very few times another researcher has e-mailed him to share ideas, Jim has felt honoured that someone else has found and read his work.

Using computers to record and organize data

Researchers are not always alone in their quests to analyze their data. A variety of computer-assisted qualitative-data-analysis software (CAQDAS) is available to help researchers code, classify, and sort qualitative data. Once mastered, these applications can save time and make analysis easier. However, they have drawbacks because they rely on generalized principles and not the specific, situational knowledge that so often lives at the heart of site-based action research.

In other words, these programs can take some of the tedium out of the stage where you are organizing your data, but they do not perform the work of analysis—that is still *your* job. Because you are most familiar with the research site and participants, your professional insights remain the most valuable perspective. For new researchers, coming to believe comfortably that their insights are valuable can be a huge stretch—this "research business" is all so new. Still, there is no denying this research fact: a person who conducts research with care and consideration is the best judge of whether the findings of that research are valid and reliable.

Qualitative researchers (especially teachers) are interested in how their research helps make life better for people (usually children). Given this central focus, it is possible to get caught up mucking around with the statistics to the extent that you lose the big picture of your project (the impact on people). It can be tempting and is sometimes appropriate to quantify or measure qualitative data, especially when some audiences are skeptical about qualitative research (sadly, skepticism is especially alive in the field of education). However, the appearance of credibility is not the same as real credibility! Statistical data are still simply another triangulated piece of the research puzzle you are trying to put together to answer the central research question that is important to you. Statistics, charts, and graphs can lend understanding—especially as you present your findings—but they cannot provide all the insight you need to plan actions that improve student engagement, learning, or achievement.

Unless you plan to make formal qualitative research a major and ongoing part of your life, we'd suggest that the time it takes to master a CAQDAS application might be better spent further "befriending" your research data. We say "befriend" because the more familiar you become with your data the more insightful your data will become for you: as Jim often says, with not much exaggeration, when he is in the middle of a research project, the data "speak to him when he drives." As Patton (2002) suggests, many researchers don't use computerized analysis simply because they need to "get physical" with their data as part of their interpretive work (p. 446). However, if you choose the computerized route for qualitative analysis (and some do), a list of data-analysis software programs can be obtained from Wikipedia (some of which are free applications). We are not denying such analysis systems provide you further insight—in fact, we believe they do—but we do offer two suggestions. Suggestion one: don't rely on these analysis systems to do all your work for you. Suggestion two: don't spend tons of money on a particular system.

Even if you don't pursue software, there is a time and place to use technology to help you collect, work on, and present your research. Careful organization and presentation of your data makes results easy to comprehend and communicate. For the purposes of your project, if you are using Microsoft Word, you already have some charting and graphing tools to create basic visuals. Spreadsheet programs such as Microsoft Excel are also simple to master for basic data presentation. We encourage you to try them out.

Computer use in research: an example

The principal and a team of school-based action researchers in a large urban high school designed a study about behaviour in the common areas of the school. The school had administrative assistants who could input the data with little cost, so data collection took the form of surveys and interviews. A basic survey, widely disseminated, provided statistical data about expectations and attitudes among students. Qualitative-data-analysis software coded key themes emerging from interviews with staff, students, and the school administrative team, and helped the research team create themes and then analyze the different responses among these groups.

The software also helped the research team translate the qualitative data into statistics, visuals, and user-friendly reports, all of which helped interpret and present the data. By making the data quantifiable, it was easier to communicate findings to stakeholders. One specific advantage was that the statistics provided a variety of persuasive charts and graphs that the school prized.

Organizing and interpreting data: a case study

Here's an example of the sort of data you might draw from a particular study, along with some suggestions about how they might be written up in a report.

Your school, located in northern Alberta, would like to create a brochure that provides parents with the "vision, mission, and goals" message the school is trying to impart, along with visuals appropriate to this message. Five years ago, the school division hired a consulting firm to create a brochure for this purpose. The school division asked you to look at this brochure and write a short report. The division is not quite happy with the brochure, but is unsure why. As one organizational leader notes, "It just seems wrong somehow."

You begin by reading carefully the brochure produced by the consulting firm. Your initial look shows you that there are several parts to the brochure. First, there is text broken into sections. For example, one section tells the history of the school; another outlines the organizational vision. Second, there are photos. Some of these photos show people working in schools, and some show education programs in action. Third, there is a series of charts that seem aimed at conveying the school's success.

You first study the language of the text and decide that it is excessively formal. This language, to you, is a problem because the booklet's readers are in rural northern Alberta. Most of them are farmers or workers on the rigs, and few have a university education. When you study the photos, you see that they don't reflect the culture and staff of the school: they show large schools in urban settings, and most of the administrators in the photos are men and Caucasian. These themes do not correspond to the school for which the brochure was written—a school with many Aboriginal students and staff, and many women administrators.

The charts are also problematic. They seem more in tune with the global than the local, and reflect the nature of education as a whole rather than painting a picture of the school and its culture. You note other things about the brochure, but the failure to engage the nature of the school has left its stamp on every page, and you sense that the consulting firm that created the brochure five years ago just simply missed the audience.

So how do you organize the data? You could write a report based on an outline something like this:

Text
- reading level (examples)
- formal language and alternatives

Photos
- gender, class, and ethnicity
- activities portrayed

Charts
- ease of comprehension
- usefulness of data presented

Once data from the brochure are used to create this basic outline, additional data from other sources can easily be incorporated into the categories. Say, for instance, someone conducted a focus group on the brochure. Comments of participants could be sorted into the categories and used to elaborate your own observations about the brochure.

How to know your findings are accurate

All researchers must ultimately ask themselves, "Can I trust my findings?" Regardless of your specific research project and data-collection methods, you can have more confidence in the accuracy of your results when you use a number of different data sources (as we recommended in Chapter 5, which focused on designing a research method). Unless they are really goofy, the use of multiple sources—triangulation—always gives you a more comprehensive picture of what you are studying.

Triangulating your data

The term *triangulation* is used quite commonly in research—and we have used it several times in this book. However, it first emerged from the daily practice of sailors and surveyors. They always measured their position in reference to another place. But it was never enough to use one or two points of reference to ascertain where they were—location was best understood by studying it as the intersection of three points. Using proper equipment and careful tools for measurement, sailors were able to circumnavigate the world, and surveyors were able to accurately draw lines and boundaries. In a world where accuracy was a life-and-death matter, being a few degrees off could mean being lost forever.

The metaphor of triangulation is useful to researchers. Researchers need solid and useful points of reference to ensure the reliability of their data. In research terms (Denzin, 1978), triangulation means that researchers use different sets of data, different types of analyses, and different theoretical perspectives to study one particular phenomenon. Different points of view help situate the research for both the researcher and the reader of that research.

Thoughtful consideration and agreement is a keystone to judgment. For this reason, juries in criminal trials are made up of more than one person.

When creating a research method or plan, a researcher carefully considers and chooses a set of data-collection methods that will help triangulate the study (as we mentioned in Chapter 5). She then uses these as points of reference to help analyze the data and explain her findings to readers. They tell readers much about how they should understand the research for themselves and how much they can generalize from this research to answer questions that arise from their own interests. As a simple example, if a researcher studies only women or children—but uses several methods to study these groups—the research may be solid and useful, but only insofar as it pertains to women and children. It would not be satisfactory to address the needs of men within an organization. The same could be said of research that is limited to positional status (e.g., school superintendents), culture (e.g., European school curricula), geography (the southern USA), or time (completed before 1975). It would be difficult to generalize widely from studies that gather data from specific contexts.

As mentioned, sailors and surveyors triangulated so that they might locate where they were in relation to other points. Similarly, in research, triangulation helps the researcher gain more credible data and make sense of the situation, activity, or participants being studied. As crucial as triangulating data might be, it's important to point out that *one* perspective in triangulation must not be forgotten: that of the person doing the research. All researchers have perspectives about the studies they are completing. That is why good qualitative research (in fact, all good research) begins with as careful a description of the researcher as possible. The sailor's location is always part of the triangulation, and the researcher's perspective is always part of the research.

Sagor (1992) describes perspectives as "independent windows" on a problem under study. We have adapted the following example from his work (p. 43). Say a researcher was studying cooperative work within a school. The researcher might study organizational documents (newsletters, staff meeting agendas, etc.), observe school functions, ask a principal to evaluate a videotape of her own performance, and interview teachers. If all these "windows" report a similar picture, that picture would likely be valid. However, if the principal rated staff meetings as useful but teachers saw them differently, that difference could trigger a further line of inquiry—a line that would have been missed without the different perspectives, and a line that

ENGAGING IN ACTION RESEARCH

might mean you revisit and adjust your research plan. Research, we have said more than once, is an iterative process—it's important to make adjustments as you learn more about what you are investigating.

As Sagor's example shows, triangulation provides more faithful findings, especially when different data sources agree. When different data sources show discrepancies, more study and data collection are required before you can have confidence in the findings. Triangulating data sources demands more planning and more data gathering to provide multiple, independent windows on the study—but, if you want your research to be credible, triangulation is essential.

About evaluating reliability and validity

When you are reading research, you will often come across the terms *reliability* and *validity*. Each of these ideas is crucial to the conduct of good research. All professional researchers believe that they should conduct research "considerately." In other words, they must address both validity and reliability.

For validity, we ask, "Does the research method do what it says it will do?"

For reliability, we ask, "Does the research method do what it says it will do every time?"

If you are conducting quantitative research, these questions are relatively easy to answer. For example, you might be testing a new literacy program that promises to help children read. Your first questions are those of validity. Does the reading program actually give positive results? That is, do children really learn how to read? The second questions concern reliability. If the program has positive results this time, will it have positive results next time? Does it work in other schools, just like it works in this school? Does it work for all children?

If your research is qualitative, the questions are a bit trickier. Because the focus of your research is the "subject" (child, teacher, or parent) not the "object" (a reading program), you must ask subjective questions about reliability and validity. For example:

- Validity: "Does what I am seeing in my research match what my professional experience suggests I should be seeing?"
- Reliability: "Does what I am describing to you about this research 'ring true' with your own experiences and understandings?"

See Table 4 for slightly different criteria and questions that are also useful for evaluating qualitative data.

Table 4. EVALUATING QUALITATIVE DATA

DATA CHARACTERISTIC	EVALUATION QUESTIONS
Credibility – authentic and believable	Is there enough detail from enough sources? Are the sources perceived as reliable?
Confirmation – internally valid	Do the people studied recognize themselves? Do the people studied agree that your themes get at important issues?
Dependability – externally valid	Do others familiar with the situation trust the data as accurate and informative? Do your findings resonate with other cases?
Transferability – applicable to other situations	Is sufficient detail present to help others who care generalize to their contexts? Can findings be generalized into a theory or model? Can findings be applied to other populations?

When you feel swamped

We can't stress enough how helpful it is to join forces with critical friends and engage each other's work—just talking to someone about what you see helps you find the words for what you are seeing. Share your work, and accept the task of both seeking and providing insights for your colleagues. We cannot tell you how many times new researchers have told us, "I really didn't know what I was thinking until I told another person."

And, with as much care as you can, create *your own* insights for *your* work. Perhaps you feel as if you are a relative rookie doing research. However, here is the truth about you and your research project: other people from other places have not gained your depth of knowledge about your site-based action research project. We are encouraging you (again) to take ownership of your work. Be confident that what you see and interpret is valuable. As the researcher, you are the expert on the data you have gathered.

Also remember that your work helps both your organization and others working in your area of study. Thus, trust your own insights about what you have done. But hold these insights tentatively. As the old Zen-like proverb goes: if you hold the bird in your hand too tightly, you will kill it; if you hold it too loosely, it will fly away. Instead hold it in a cupped hand, both firmly and gently at the same time.

Finally, we emphasize the importance of being systematic in your attention to detail for data collection. Work hard to set up regular times (even short times) to reflect and consider what is happening in your work. Write your thoughts down and collect them somewhere where you won't lose them. Remember that analysis is a slow and thoughtful process. Over time, small, short visits with your data will lend deeper and richer insights than panicky marathon sessions. Schedule these visits, and leave time and space between so your ideas and insights can form.

In a recently reviewed online journal of a man travelling, day by day, through Argentina, the traveller summarized his experience of one day by saying *poco a poco se va lejos*—"little by little, one goes far." We think this also sums up the experience of completing site-based action research.

10

Reporting your findings

ESSENTIAL QUESTIONS
What is the purpose of a research report?
How can you structure your research report to clearly communicate your findings?

CHAPTER PURPOSE
To examine the basic structure of a research report
To share tips and advice to consider when reporting your research findings to a larger audience

Reporting your findings in a comprehensive and clear way can be challenging. In the movie *Dragnet*, Sergeant Joe Friday (played by Canadian actor Dan Aykroyd) often requests "Just the facts, ma'am." But what are the facts?

The answer is that "Just the facts, ma'am" doesn't fit action research. Reporting action research is different from reporting "factual" information. The data that emerge from site-based action research must be transformed into a narrative. The report is primarily a story about what you have found and what you believe these findings mean. Your challenge, as an author of action research, is to understand and report (1) your findings, (2) the conditions under which these findings were uncovered, and (3) the knowledge and insights you have come to discover as you have engaged in the entire research process.

A research report is an open story about the past, written in the present. It is not like looking in the mirror and seeing the past reflected perfectly to your eyes. Research is about creating meaning from data—data, on their own, do not have meaning. So, research reports assume different shapes and different spins, and storytellers like yourself create these spins as you strive to make sense of what happened during your research. A research report is a story based on good judgment. In the end, you must ask yourself whether it presents a realistic account of what happened.

Your final report: the story of your research

Today's postmodern perspectives challenge the empirical-analytical belief that research findings can represent a universally understood set of *correct* facts. We do not believe that everyone who experiences the same event will gain the same insights; we believe events generate as many perspectives as there are witnesses and participants. This means that your research report will describe *your* sense of what *you* have done and how *your* participants understood what was done. It will be *your story*—not something objective and universal, but something conscientious, truthful, and personal about what happened.

About empiricism

Empiricism is the philosophical belief that all knowledge is derived from experience. Quantitative research relies on experiences you receive from the outside world through your senses, such as your sense of sight or smell. Qualitative research includes other experiences as well: your inner experiences. For example, what thoughts and feelings occur when you hear a particular song that was meaningful to you in the past, or when you smell an aroma that reminds you of the pies your mom used to bake? Qualitative research recognizes that we gain experience (and knowledge) both from the outside world via our senses and from the inner world of thoughts and reflections. As an action (qualitative) researcher, this means that your research report should include thoughts and reflections—yours and others'. These form part of the empirical context of your research, and are important to better understanding your work.

Empirical knowledge comes from both inside and outside, from both self and others. These dual centres of understanding are important to gaining a better understanding of your research— part of triangulation, as we discussed in Chapter 9—and they are key to generating knowledge from your research. As empiricism suggests, knowledge involves constructing the general from the particular.

Qualitative research uses a different set of cognitive processes to generate knowledge than quantitative research. These processes seek to expand the context of understanding, rather than replicate particular results. Morse (1994) identifies four cognitive processes integral to all qualitative studies:

- comprehending—the attempt to search for and learn everything possible about the setting, the culture, and the study topic
- synthesizing—the merging of stories, experiences, or cases that describe the patterns or responses of the participants
- theorizing—the development and manipulation of theoretical ideas until the most fruitful is developed
- recontextualizing—the development of theory that might apply to other settings

About objectivity

For many quantitative researchers, objectivity is fundamental to good analysis. However, objectivity doesn't fit well with the more fluid and qualitative nature of the site-based action research in which teachers engage. Trying to be objective doesn't work for two reasons. First, as we noted in Chapter 2, it is impossible for you to be objective—and why would you want to be? So many of our human experiences have little to do with logic and objectivity and much more to do with relationships, which are powerfully *subjective*. For this reason, the number of qualitative research studies in the social sciences has grown. Almost all thorough current research studies in the social sciences are "mixed methods" in their approach—that is, they include both quantitative and qualitative analyses.

Believing there can be no *one* truth requires action researchers to create meaning from their work by engaging a variety of possible, legitimate interpretations of what happened. These interpretations become the "story" of the research you have completed. As an action researcher, you have little choice but to use narratives to share the knowledge you have gained from your research. And, by using narratives, you accept that your research is authored by you—a person who holds deep interests in the research she is authoring.

Action research is less about reporting objective discoveries, and more about relating personal insights into what happened. (For a summary of the differences between reporting for quantitative research and action research, see Table 5.) Your writing, as an action researcher, is like the activity of an author, and you create a text based on the most sensible meanings you can garner from the evidence you've gathered. This process is complex, personal, and directed by sensible choices.

Table 5. COMPARING TYPES OF RESEARCH REPORTING

Quantitative research reporting	Action research reporting
Objective	Subjective
- works toward scientific truth	- provides multiple perspectives
- attempts to erase researcher bias from research	- accepts researcher bias as part of the research
- uses a dispassionate, third-person writing style	- often uses a first-person narrative writing style (personal report style)
- discounts feelings and nuances as a source of bias that should not enter the reporting process	- documents feelings and nuances to help the reader understand, relate to, and appreciate the issue under study
- trusted when its methods produce the same results under the same conditions (factual proof)	- trusted when it speaks to a "shared reality"

As you craft your final research report, consider these four questions:

- What assumptions do you bring to your work?
- How do these assumptions shape how you construct your research narrative and insights?
- What will you do with what you have come to know?
- How will you represent the answers to the three previous questions to the public?

These questions will shape your research report. Answering these questions puts you in line with others whose ultimate goal is to identify and promote ways in which individuals at the cutting edge of their professions can carry out work that is ethical and socially responsible.

Organizing your research report

Research reports allow researchers to share findings with others. They aim to communicate. Approaches to reporting vary, but reports should be comprehensive and allow outsiders to follow the research process (Gummesson, 2000).

Most research reports include similar sections. Here are the sections Stringer (1999, p. 174) outlines for a typical research report:

Introduction: identifies the problem or presents the question

Literature review: details what is known about the problem

Methodology: discusses research design and data collection

Results: provides a summary of data analysis

Conclusion: identifies the practical implications of the study

Beyond a formal report, there are a number of ways to tell the story of your research so that others can benefit from your work for their own professional development. Ways of sharing could include:

- articles for newsletters or teacher magazines
- staff meetings
- conversations with colleagues
- blogs
- work within your professional association

Reports: a section-by-section breakdown

We encourage you to contemplate the breakdown we present here before you write your report. Your organization may provide a specific structure for you to follow, and the audience you are writing for will also determine your report's final shape and content. Regardless, we believe a standard breakdown—like the one that follows—will allow you to be more confident as you proceed on this final leg of your research journey.

The questions we present here can help you develop your research story—the core of your report, whatever its ultimate structure. They aim to prompt you to think about the context of your work: the factors that have shaped your findings. In qualitative research, discussing context is as important as discussing findings. A clear presentation of a wide range of factors will inform your reader, and will likely help you discover connections in your own work—those "light bulb" moments—as you write. Enjoy writing. Your research report will be the fruition of a great deal of hard work. It is your story to tell!

SECTION I PURPOSE OF THE RESEARCH PROJECT

- What was your research project about? Provide a general but engaging introduction.
- What generated your interest in this project?
- What area or problem does your research project address?
- Why is your research project important?
- How does your project fit with other work, knowledge, or other research projects in your area, school, or division?

This section introduces the reader to your research. We believe this first section works best when it is personal and when it gives reasons as to why you are interested in the problem you have chosen to investigate. If possible, tell a story. Why do you care about the problem? What got you interested in the first place? What did you hope to accomplish, and what do you anticipate being able to do with the results of your research? In short, describe your personal interest in your problem.

You may also discuss the significance of your work. The impact or significance of the research justifies why your research project is important and how it seeks to address a real educational problem. In this section, describe the potential impact if the problem is not eliminated or solved. Again, write in the first person, but be sure to answer the fundamental question of why others (not just you) should care about what you have been investigating. If someone asked you "So what?" how would you answer?

SECTION II RESEARCH QUESTION

- What is the central research question that guided your data collection?
- What subquestions did you address to answer your central research question?

This section states the questions your research project tried to answer. Again, the style of this section should be personal, so write in the first person. The main research question and subquestions should be in bullet form.

SECTION III CONCEPTUAL FRAMEWORK

- What conceptual framework have you adopted in producing your report? Simply stated, where are you coming from?
- What theoretical perspective or practical stance are you assuming?

Remember that, earlier in this chapter, we spoke about biases that come with the researcher. As well as you can, describe your biases— where you are coming from. The more clearly you can describe yourself as a researcher, the more clearly another person can understand your work and how it might be applied to another situation.

For example: "I have been a grade-one teacher for twenty-six years in an urban school. In my research project, I have attempted to seek best practices for teaching and leadership." Be as explicit as you can.

SECTION IV RESEARCH SITE

- What are the characteristics of your situation? How might these differ from other sites?
- What are the characteristics of the people you worked with? How are these unique?
- What else can you tell us about the "where" of the site you used for your research?

Describe and review information that will help the reader better know the unique situation in which you have been working. For example, rural areas differ from urban areas. Your project might focus on at-risk children in elementary school who are, of course, different from high-achieving high school students. Try to provide insight into both the specifics of your site and its culture. Any information presented here should amplify or support the description of the problem that triggered your research. In short, tell about the place of your site-based action research project.

As well, tell the reader about the people who were the project participants. Respectful of confidentiality, describe but do not identify the people who participated in your research. This list and explanation should include anyone on the "doing" side of the study and anyone on the participation side of the study. Identify and talk about those on your project team. Without violating anyone's (or any group's) research ethics, describe your participants in as much detail as possible. Remember, your goal is to help people who read your study understand how context and people might have influenced findings (it is not to gossip about anyone).

SECTION V LITERATURE REVIEW

- What key literature has helped you build your understanding of your chosen topic?
- How does this literature fit what you have found out during your own research?

We discussed the process of completing a literature review in Chapter 4. This is where your literature review goes. It should summarize, describe, and critique published research that is similar in focus to your own research. You should also outline the insights provided by this research that might be relevant to your own work. Stick to professional, published research here—not opinions. Your sources should be journals, peer-reviewed articles, books, and other recognized sources of information.

SECTION VI RESEARCH METHOD

- In what ways was your research quantitative or qualitative in character?
- How did you collect your data? (Be specific. For example, did you use focus groups, interviews, document analysis?)
- Why did you choose to conduct your research as you did? How do your data-collection methods fit your research objectives?

This section should outline your research method (research plan), something we discussed in detail in Chapter 5. The goal is to explain what you did so others might replicate your work.

Don't forget that there is a difference between a research methodology and your research method. When you write about your research methodology, tell whether your approach was quantitative, qualitative, or mixed (using both qualitative and quantitative strategies). Give reasons why the methodology you selected was the most appropriate to address the questions your research study hoped to answer.

When you write about your research method, outline your data-collection methods—that is, the specific steps you took to collect your data (your "research lesson plan"). Specifically summarize the sample of participants you used. Discuss the instruments you used (tests, measures, observations, scales, and surveys you employed to answer your research questions), including how you employed or distributed the instruments, any instructions you gave your participants as part of using the instruments, and how you collected and recorded the data the instruments generated. Describe the steps you used to analyze your data and explain in detail any statistical or qualitative analysis you used.

SECTION VII RESEARCH PROJECT SCOPE

- What were the delimitations of your research project?
- What key assumptions have you made that allowed you to proceed with your research?
- What terms do you need to define in your research?

Think of this section as where you set out the terms of reference for your study—what your readers need to know about the limits you deliberately placed on your research, the assumptions you deliberately made to move forward, and the terminology you need to use to describe it.

Research delimitations are factors under your control. For example, to make your study manageable, you might have chosen to look only at teachers in a particular city or county. Or, in a study of the behaviours of teacher coaches, you might have chosen to delimit your interviews to three coaches you believed were able to answer the questions you hoped to answer. By delimiting your study, you will have missed some data. However, if you have delimited your study wisely, you will have enough data to answer your central research question. List the boundaries you placed on your research by stating: "To make my research manageable, I chose to delimit it in certain ways. The delimitations of my study were..."

You should also consider the limits of what you can do with, or say about, your findings. It is better to be humble than to overreach your findings. That said, if you have come to understand or believe something as a result of your research, don't be afraid to throw it out there so others can engage it. There is a difference between being speculative (a good thing) and being arrogantly overconfident (a bad thing). Share courageously what you believe you have found, but note in what ways your work is limited in its reach.

Research assumptions are ideas that you had to assume to conduct your work. For example, if your research used a survey, you must assume that respondents answered truthfully. If you used a focus group, you must assume that focus-group members are representative of the larger group of teachers you might have chosen.

List your assumptions by stating: "To complete my research, I made the following assumptions…"

Terminology has an important role in every kind of research. It matters how you use and define specific terms. Such terms can be conceptual (how you might define *student achievement* or *good schools*, for example), or operational (what *teacher coaching* means in a particular site). Define all the important terms that are crucial to your study. When you are in doubt, it does not hurt to "over define."

In addition, be clear and transparent. For example, some terms and phrases, in different situations, mean completely different things. Clearly define any terms, situations, or events that another person, unfamiliar with the situation, might not understand. State: "To understand my research more completely, the following terms must be defined…" Define these terms as if you were writing a glossary.

SECTION VIII RESEARCH ETHICS

- What ethical considerations were part of your study?
- How did you protect your participants?
- How did you safeguard your data?

As a researcher, you must act to protect your participants as well as do things as ethically as you can—just because doing things well is the right way to live. Bogdan and Biklen (1992) suggest that two ethical considerations exist in any research with human subjects: (1) *informed consent*—participants must enter the study voluntarily while understanding the nature of the study, its potential dangers, and their obligations; and (2) *protection of subjects from harm*—subjects should not be exposed to risks greater than the gains they might derive from their participation in the study.

Every research project should concern itself with protecting anonymity and confidentiality: it should provide participants the freedom to leave the study, share important data, check meanings, and so on. How have you addressed these ethical considerations? If you have not, why were these considerations not applicable?

SECTION IX RESULTS

- What are your findings?
- What did you discover from your research?

If you have kept a research journal in some form—a running collection of your thoughts as your research proceeded—this is where it can be especially helpful. Consider the observations you have made, and ideas you have come up with, along your research journey. Use those ideas and understandings to answer the *What?* question (in later sections of your report, you'll get to the *So what?* and the *Now what?* questions). Describe what you have discovered through your journaling. Simply, what story has your research led you to want to tell? Remember to link your findings to evidence. Be as specific as possible.

Keep in mind, however, that research never proves anything. Regardless of how well you have done your research, you will never be able to say that you *proved* something or that you have discovered the truth. As we have noted in this chapter, research never deals in absolute truths and proofs. Research *suggests* actions rather than *orders* them.

SECTION X CONCLUSIONS

- What conclusions have you made based on your research findings?
- What recommendations can you make specific to your findings and your conclusions?

In this section, state the conclusions you have reached. Support your conclusions with evidence from your findings, and link your findings to the findings of other research studies you have read.

We encourage you to trust that you have something valuable to say. You will have gained tremendous knowledge and understanding of your area through your research. Dare to make recommendations, but base these specifically on your findings and conclusions. Be clear how any recommendations can be supported by what you found during the conduct of your site-based action research.

SECTION XI IMPLICATIONS

- What might your research mean for the future of educational practice? What does it suggest educators might do to improve student learning?
- How can your research benefit students in classrooms?

This section describes the *So what?* outcomes of your project. Now that you have completed your research, what does your work mean? There are two aspects of the *So what?* question.

Begin by asking, "What should happen in my educational site as a result of my work?" Think about your starting points. As a site-based action researcher, a question about improving student engagement, learning, and/or achievement probably lay at the foundation of your research project. Now you need to answer it: How can students benefit from your research? List any recommended changes that could improve your place of work and detail how the implementation process might happen. What changes do you believe should be made? What are the implications of not making these changes? If you have designed a tool or process for intervention as a result of your research—for example, a workshop series, an evaluation protocol, a new curriculum outline—describe and explain it here.

Next, ask the *Now what?* question. What other research do you think should be done to extend your work? You are now part of the full-on, professional research conversations that engage your topic of interest. In this section, step up and take your place in that dialogue.

SECTION XII REFLECTIONS ON THE PROCESS

- What lessons have you learned from this process?

In this section, your aim is to take your place among academic scholars and to help future researchers avoid pitfalls in any research they might later do.

As you worked through your site-based action research project, undoubtedly you came to see that you could have done some things differently. This discovery is typical. Perhaps you saw that you had missed a promising possibility for further study, but you simply didn't have time to pursue it. Describe how you might proceed if you were to do the study again. Describe the implications of your research for the body of knowledge you have studied.

You might also consider reviewing the conduct and management of your research project. Identify what you could have done better or what processes you would now change.

Hints for report writing

Hint 1: If there is a choice between writing short and writing long, write short.

Hint 2: If there is a choice between writing clearly or confoundingly, write clearly.

Hint 3: Use your energy wisely. Use your colleagues as resources, and offer yourself as a useful colleague. You have everything you need to do the job—so work systematically and with others to complete it.

Hint 4: Although the sections will weave together, a report is a group of pieces. Just follow a template—the one in this chapter or one that better suits your needs. There is no one right answer.

Hint 5: Finish the report one piece at a time. Don't get swallowed up by the whole forest. Chop this tree, clear this bush, move it from the path, move to the next tree or bush. Likely, you will discover ideas and connections that open up new avenues as you write. Follow them as they reveal themselves, but begin the process by following the path outlined in your template. If your own writing takes you to a dead end, return to that template path again.

Hint 6: Use your infrastructure of critical friends. Get together with other teachers and colleagues to read and comment on each other's work—literally and figuratively. Make writing your research report a social, community activity. Help yourself by helping each other.

11

Pacing yourself

ESSENTIAL QUESTIONS
How can new researchers sustain their work? What work needs should they keep in mind?
What can you do if things go wrong?

CHAPTER PURPOSE
To share our experiences with sustaining our own work
To provide tips for beginning researchers that might positively impact their research

We encourage you to read through this chapter (and all the chapters of this book) before you begin your work. This chapter presents important considerations for anyone who really wants to complete a research project.

These considerations touch on less formal aspects of your work as an action researcher. We describe them as needs you will face, and suggest strategies to respond to them. We know these needs from our own work as researchers—from our collective experiences doing research, teaching research, and sustaining research activity.

Know your work needs

Many new researchers are anxious to begin their work as soon as they have designed their research method. Nothing prevents you from doing this. However, our experience suggests your enthusiasm and energy can flag if you take on too much work too soon. Anticipating your needs will help you pace and sustain yourself.

Need 1: Staying organized

Teachers are busy! Like your peers, you are no doubt juggling family and work responsibilities. With so much going on, at times it can be difficult to stay organized and focused, particularly without externally imposed deadlines. Most of us are great at meeting deadlines when someone else assigns them, but less able to meet them when no one is looking over our shoulders. New researchers often struggle with the wide-open space research offers. That is why, earlier, we encouraged you to outline the steps in your research method and overall project with specificity and with a timeline. That timeline—your research and project schedule—forms the basis of your time management as you complete your work. We recommend using a calendar to clearly post your research project's milestones.

At the risk of banality, we also remind you of the story *The Tortoise and the Hare.* You'll remember Aesop concluded that "Slow but steady wins the race." Lawyer and best-selling author John Grisham took three years to complete his first novel, *A Time to Kill*—three years of getting up at 5:00 in the morning six days a week, writing an hour or two at a time. We have found that small blocks of regularly scheduled time add up to project completion.

We encourage you to break big jobs into little pieces you can accomplish in an hour at a time. Most of our writing on this book, for example, was done in short time sessions. All these little sessions added up. To finish your research project, we encourage you to set aside regular times each week to work. Scheduled activities can include writing or formatting your final report, reviewing literature, revisiting your research plan, entering research-journal notes, making project-related phone calls, creating electronic files and e-mails, or scheduling activities and appointments. There is much to do that extends past writing.

Need 2: Sustaining energy

We encourage you to stay your course. But you also need to rest. Here's our question: How can researchers rest and work at the same time? Over our years of researching, we have come up with some solutions that work for us.

Multitask the little things. You may be a person who needs to do one thing at a time, but if you get tired of that one thing, we suggest having something—perhaps something rather mindless—to do when you just need a break. You may want to make a to-do list or job jar, and write all those little things—such as alphabetizing your reference list—that you just need to do. These tasks might not take much time, but they are to-dos that you simply have *to do*.

In our work life, when we need a break from the deep thinking or the routine of one kind of work, we stop to do something different. But we never quit working. We simply move to the other work that must be done at some point. So, make a list and turn to it when you are tired of other stuff.

Add to your review of literature. We believe that you should work hard to complete your literature review early in your work. However, we also believe you can kind of have it both ways: both finish it early and put it off. When you need a little vacation in the middle of your work, stop and go back to research literature you didn't get to. Or, do a simple online search for two or three—understand that this means only two or three—articles that you might add to your literature review. This practical tactic shows you how your thinking is changing and maturing as you have been working on your research project. We have found that such a literature "trip" can actually revitalize both us and our work.

Help your colleagues. We have often noted in this book the great treasure colleagues can be. We encourage you to build a professional learning network that works together regularly. Such small networks of teachers are both helpful and restful. Some of the best partnerships we know involve colleagues actively and systematically meeting online to work through and read each other's material. This arrangement must be win-win, but when such partnerships work, they really work!

Need 3: Keeping notes

Keep notes. Somehow, in some way, learn to keep systematic notes about your work. We encourage you to either (1) do formal journaling or (2) create a regular e-mailing system where you can share your research work. We encourage you to e-mail your notes to a friend and keep a copy for yourself. There are three reasons for adopting a note-taking strategy: it aids your research; it helps with your personal development as a researcher; and it aids with self-care. It is a way to track your own ideas and thoughts, and it provides a time of solitude and reflection that we all need.

Save the notes. Somehow, in a form that works for you, figure out how to bank your reflections and notes in a way that will serve as a data source at a later time. We strongly encourage you to think ahead and visualize how you might analyze your data, and set up a storage and retrieval system that will work for you. Don't forget to store notes safely and confidentially.

Revel in the notes. Before you begin to write your final research report, we encourage you to review your notes slowly. Sit down with a nice cup of tea or a glass of wine, and simply read through your notes. First, read them for a general sense of what they say. Second, read them for specific themes that might emerge. Third, read them for specific examples that will help your work. Notice how many research processes are redundant!

Need 4: Rewriting and editing

We have found over our years as researchers that we love to write, and seek opportunities to do so. However, you may not share our enthusiasm—you may find writing as much fun as having a root canal. We suggest that, rather than procrastinating and then trying to finish the whole project report in the final weeks before a deadline, make writing a normal and integral part of your project work.

Start writing now. It might seem odd to begin writing before you have started to conduct your research, but when you go back and look at your project overview (which we discussed in Chapter 7), you will see that there are all sorts of areas you can work on to build your final research report. Jim always encourages the researchers he works with to immediately begin shaping material from the overview into the final writing. Doing this provides a sense of accomplishment and actually gets the work done. For now, even if it is not your nature, become a pack rat. Save everything in a designated spot. If you are like others, you will find it less daunting—perhaps even encouraging—to have a rough draft started in advance.

Outline, outline, outline. Outlines are the maps (or dreams) of finished projects. They are quicker and easier to play with, revise, and organize than reams of meandering text. We suggest you draft an outline of your work early and continue to revisit and revise this outline as your project takes shape. If you get lost and no longer can remember what—or why—you are writing, go back and review your outline. Play with it; think about it; use it as a tool to help you visualize the big picture.

Break it down. Writing is hard work, as you probably already know. We encourage you to write until your brain gets tired—no more. Writing for a half-hour to an hour at a time is better than not writing at all. Many people never become writers because they think they *should* be able to write for hours. In our experience, marathon (especially last-day) writing sessions are less productive or creative than short, well-paced bursts.

Do lots of write-throughs. When we say "write-throughs," we mean starting at the beginning and reading your work while, at the same time, making small edits to the work. Some people seem to sweat bullets while they are writing. They sit in front of their computer

ENGAGING IN ACTION RESEARCH

screen barely able to squeeze out any words at all. What stops them, we believe, is that they are trying to do all the writing tasks—organizing, outlining, making words, and final editing—all at once. A more fruitful way to write is to split up the work into component parts and then do only one part at a time.

In our own work, we sometimes do 10 to 15 write-throughs. Every time, we make a little change here, a tweak there, a few additions and subtractions everywhere we can. We never worry about the final edit until the final edit arrives, and then, because we have already been through the work so often, the final edit is easy. We encourage you to write one piece at a time—not too much, just a little. Don't worry—you can always come back and fix something.

Know when to call in reinforcements. It almost seems pro forma for some teachers to hire outside editors. We believe outside editing is usually unnecessary. There are only a few times when you need this extreme move. Honestly, if you are a decent writer and have a colleague with whom you have a working arrangement (a reading agreement), you do not need to hire an outside editor. However, if you are not a good writer—if you are, in fact, a poor writer (that does not make you a bad person)—then you might consider hiring an editor. But if you have a colleague who can fulfill this role, we say don't hire an editor.

Do your APA style right the first time. APA style (writing protocols of the American Psychological Association) is a given—some say a necessary evil—of academic work in the social sciences. Stylistic conventions form their own language and grammar, and these are necessary. They help people in the academic community speak clearly to one another about what they have learned. Frankly, APA style is easy enough to work with once you've mastered the basics. We strongly recommend that you learn these basics and do it right the first time. Correcting mistakes in APA is tedious, time-consuming, and frustrating—especially because teachers may leave these until the last minute.

Avoid the whole mess of revising your work by consulting an APA guide, as you need it. The areas you most need to concern yourself with are (1) providing proper references in your reference list and (2) using in-text citations properly in the body of your work. You can buy the APA style guide if you want, but you can also try one or more of these ideas:

- Study and copy the style of references used in reliable documents that use APA style. The keyword here is *reliable*—make sure the work you use is a resource written by someone who knew her stuff.

- Consult the library. Remember that most university libraries have good systems for helping people complete their projects, and they usually charge nothing for their services. This includes stylistic advice. Don't take advantage of them (i.e., do your work well), but do take advantage of them—does that make sense?
- Consult online style guides. Almost every university library has a condensed version of APA style basics among its support documents. These online guides are often more succinct and easier to use than the actual APA style guide. Find a good one that you can easily refer to quickly, bookmark it, and use it as you write. We use the Purdue Online Writing Lab (OWL), which is free.

Need 5: Drawing support from your network

Most researchers have a network of people there to help them. These include people in their organization, their colleagues, and family or friends. We encourage you to use the members of your network and to become a member of someone else's network as well. Use, but don't abuse—that is a key concept. In our experience, it's rare to see abuse or *over*use of networks. Most teacher researchers do not use their networks as well as they could. Your network has good people who want to help in any way they can. And, in our experience, these people are both useful and helpful. Don't be afraid to ask for any help they can give.

However, we also encourage you to ask nicely. Some teachers become so wrapped up in their projects that they forget other people have lives. Ask how your support people work best, and negotiate an arrangement that works for everyone. Respect the limits of that arrangement. For example, don't expect immediate feedback. If you get immediate feedback, you are fortunate; but most people are part-time supports who must fit this work around their own work.

If things go wrong

It is wise to ask, "What can go wrong?" and "How can anything that goes wrong be fixed?"

Home and life issues might complicate things. Sometimes life conspires to make completing your research project difficult. We cannot even imagine what might happen in your life. Something extraordinary occurs that halts the process. You become ill. You move. Your marriage breaks up. While it is impossible to list every example, our overall advice is to let your network and your project team know what is going on, and to work out a solution. These things happen to people, and perhaps the first thing to realize is that you are not alone. People do figure out a way through, and so can you.

Your research itself might become an issue. Some teachers come to believe that their project is just not working. Perhaps you believe you had too few survey responses. Perhaps the anticipated help was not forthcoming. Perhaps anticipated results simply did not surface. And, perhaps you have come to believe you simply were wrong. All these issues can be worked through, and usually with less difficulty than you might think. In our experience, more projects need retooling than not. Most shape-shift and become something at least slightly different from what you described in the project overview. And, most shifts are minor. Don't panic! Just work out a solution.

If your research project simply was wrong, do you still have a project? The answer is yes. Jim's mentor at the University of Texas was O. L. Davis, who two years in a row won the most prestigious researcher award from the National Council of Social Studies. O. L. was fond of saying that some of the best research reports were those where the research did not work. Why? Because such research tells us what we should *not* do. If your research didn't work, report that it didn't work. This knowledge adds to the literature in positive ways. Finally, remember that your project can change.

Final thoughts

Have you considered the magnitude of what you are doing in your site-based action research project? Your work has entered the realm of scholarship. You are working to be one of the people whose project will be soon cited as part of the "literature." Literary critic Northrop Frye (1980) wrote a short monograph titled *Creation and Recreation* in which he discussed the godlike human "pulls" in all of us that draw us to revel in our creations. Revelling in creation is the real celebration of your project. You are creating something new.

When you create something new as a result of your research, it is yours. Unless you explicitly agree that copyright in your work will belong to someone else, it belongs to you. Even if you agree to give up copyright, you have moral rights including the right to be named as the author of your work, unless you explicitly waive those rights. Finally, we encourage you to remember there are two projects. The first is your actual project—the one you proposed to do. Do it well and ethically. Second, you are the project. You are becoming a scholar who creates intellectual property. Accept that the territory comes with certain responsibilities and duties. We encourage you to do your work with celebration and seriousness.

References

Alberta Teachers' Association (2000). *Action research guide for Alberta teachers*. Edmonton: Alberta Teachers' Association. Available from http://www.teachers.ab.ca/SiteCollectionDocuments/ATA/Publications/ Professional-Development/ActionResearch.pdf

Bogdan, R.C., & Biklen, S.K. (1992). *Qualitative research in education: An introduction to theory and methods* (2nd ed.). Boston: Allyn and Bacon.

Bryson, J., & Anderson, S. (2000). Applying large-group interaction methods in the planning and implementation of major change efforts. *Public Administration Review, 60*(2), 143–162. http://dx.doi.org/10.1111 /0033-3352.00073

Canfield, J., & Switzer, J. (2005). *The success principles: How to get from where you are to where you want to be.* New York: HarperCollins.

Corsaro, W.A. (1985). *Friendship and peer culture in the early years.* New Jersey: Ablex.

Creswell, J.W. (2009). *Quantitative, and Mixed Methods Approaches* (3rd ed.). Los Angeles: Sage.

Denzin, N.K. (1978). *The research act* (2nd ed.). New York: McGraw-Hill.

Fenwick, T., & Parsons, J. (2009). *The Art of Evaluation: A Resource for Educators and Trainers* (2nd ed.). Toronto, Ontario: Thompson Educational Publishing.

Fontana, A., & Frey, J.H. (1994). Interviewing: the art of science. In N.K. Denzin & Y.S. Lincoln (Eds.), *Handbook of qualitative research* (pp. 361–376). Thousand Oaks, CA: Sage.

Freire, P. (1995). *Pedagogy of hope: Reliving pedagogy of the oppressed.* New York: Continuum.

Frye, N. (1980). *Creation and recreation.* Toronto, ON: University of Toronto Press.

Fullan, M. (2010). *Motion leadership: The skinny on becoming change savvy.* Thousand Oaks, CA: Corwin.

Glanz, J. (1998). *Action research: An educational leader's guide to school improvement.* Norwood, MA: Christopher Gordon Publishers.

Glesne, C., & Peshkin, A. (1992). *Becoming qualitative researchers: An introduction*. White Plains, NY: Longman.

Gummesson, E. (2000). *Qualitative methods in management research*. Thousand Oaks, CA: Sage Publications.

Jick, T.D. (1979). Mixing qualitative and quantitative methods: Triangulation in action. *Administrative Science Quarterly, 24*(4), 602–611. http://dx.doi .org/10.2307/2392366

Jones, S. (1985). Depth interviewing. In R. Walker (Ed.), *Applied Qualitative Research* (pp. 45–55). Aldershot: Gower.

Marsh, P., Rosser, E., & Harre, R. (1978). *The rules of disorder*. London: Routledge.

Miles, M.B., & Huberman, A.M. (1984). Drawing valid meaning from qualitative data: Toward a shared craft. *Educational Researcher, 13*(5), 20–30.

Miles, M.B., & Huberman, A.M. (1994). *Qualitative data analysis* (2nd ed.). Thousand Oaks, CA: Sage.

Morgan, D.L. (1988). *Focus groups as qualitative research*. Newbury Park, CA: Sage.

Morse, J.M. (1994). Emerging from the data: The cognitive processes of analysis in qualitative inquiry. In J.M. Morse (Ed.), *Critical issues in qualitative research methods* (pp. 23–43). Thousand Oaks, CA: Sage Publications.

National Staff Development Council. (2000). *Tools for schools*. Oxford, OH: NSDC.

Organization for Economic Development and Cooperation. (2002). *Frascati Manual: Proposed standard practice for surveys on research and experimental development*. Paris: OECD Publishing.

Owen, H. (1997). *Expanding our now: The story of open space technology*. San Francisco: Berrett-Koehler.

Parsons, J., & Beauchamp, L. (2011). *Reflecting on leadership for learning: Case studies of five Alberta elementary school principals*. Edmonton, AB: The Alberta Teachers' Association.

Patton, M.Q. (2002). *Qualitative research and research methods* (3rd ed.). Thousand Oaks, CA: Sage.

Project Management Institute Educational Foundation. (2012). *Project Management: A proven process for success*. Retrieved from http://www .pmi.org/pmief/learningzone/provenprocess.asp

Punch, K.F. (2009). *Introduction to research methods in education*. Thousand Oaks, CA: Sage.

Sagor, R. (1992). *How to conduct collaborative action research*. Alexandria, VA: ASCD.

Sagor, R. (2000). *Guiding school improvement with action research*. Alexandria, VA: Association for Supervision and Curriculum Development.

Spiller, E. (2004). *Science, reading, and renaissance Literature: The art of making knowledge, 1580–1670.* Cambridge: Cambridge University Press. http://dx.doi.org/10.1017/CBO9780511484018

Stringer, E. (1999). *Action research.* Thousand Oaks, CA: Sage Publications.

Taylor, D. (2001). *Writing a literature review.* Retrieved from http://www.google.com/url?sa=t&rct=j&q=&esrc=s&source=web&cd=1&sqi=2&ved=0C CIQFjAA&url=http%3A%2F%2Fweb.pdx.edu%2F~wooster%2FEC_Writing% 2FA%2520Literature%2520Review.

Vaill, P.B. (1996). *Learning as a way of being: Strategies for survival in a world of permanent white water.* San Francisco: Jossey-Bass.